Lessons for Little Ones

Language Arts

Cooperative Learning Lessons

Lorna Curran
In consultation with Dr. Spencer Kagan

Kagan

Kagan Publishing
1160 Calle Cordillera
San Clemente, CA 92673
1(800) WEE CO-OP
www.KaganOnline.com

ISBN: 1-879097-09-5

Table of Social Skills

Lesson Number

Social Skill	1	2	3	4	5	6	7	8	9	10	11	12	13	14	15	16	17	18	19	20	21	22	23	24	25	26	27	28	29	30	31	32	33	34	35	36
Accepting Suggestions/ Opinions Politely	●								●				●																	●						
Active Listening			●		●		●				●					●								●											●	
Encouraging Statements																												●								
Everyone Participates												●						●											●					●		
Happy Talk											●					●								●			●				●	●				
Paraphrasing						●															●															
Pass Papers Politely															●																					
Polite Suggestions													●					●	●				●													●
Strong Voices		●								●																										
Take Turns			●							●				●			●																			
Quick Work																							●			●	●									
Quiet Voices				●				●												●	●					●										

Lorna Curran: *Lessons for Little Ones: Language Arts*©
Kagan Cooperative Learning • 1 (800) Wee Co-op

by
Spencer
Kagan, Ph.D.

Foreword

For the last ten years I have been giving workshops in Cooperative Learning. Whenever the workshops have included Kindergarten through second grade teachers, the question always comes up: How do you adapt these powerful methods for use with students who do not write, have limited attention spans, and few social skills? At first, I simply said that you use the simpler structures, take it very slowly, and adapt. The K-2 teachers were almost always very kind; they did not protest, went through the workshops, and did what they could with the methods. We all knew however, that something more was needed. As I did demo lessons at various grade levels and found myself quite anxious before entering the K-2 classrooms, I knew much more was needed.

What Lorna Curran provides in this book is a giant step toward bringing successful Cooperative Learning to K-2 classrooms. Although the bulk of the book consists of three dozen lessons, the book itself provides much of what has been missing. It is a framework for Cooperative Learning for little ones. In a number of very important ways Lorna departs from the model of Cooperative Learning which I favor for students beyond second grade.

Social Skills

If you contrast the lessons in this book with those provided by others using a structural approach[1] the most noticeable difference is the tremendous emphasis on social skills. Those working with me in the structural approach for grades two and above have found success with a "natural approach" to social skills which involves choosing a "Social Skill of the Week." The Skill-of-the-Week approach fosters the development of one skill each week by the use of structures and structuring, modeling, rotating role-assignments, and reflection and planning time. With this approach, the skills are acquired as students do their math, science, language arts, and social studies with little time off the academic curriculum.

Lorna's approach for the little ones is dramatically different. Each lesson defines a distinct social skill, and the skill is emphasized through a range of methods. In fact in some of the lessons, the social skill gets more emphasis than the academic content. There are two very important reasons for this very heavy emphasis on social skill development in

1. See Jeanne Stone, *Cooperative Learning and Language Arts: A Multi-Structural Approach* and Beth Andrini, *Cooperative Learning and Math: A Multi-Structural Approach.*

K-2 classrooms. First, for the youngest students it is not enough simply to describe skills or assign roles; young students need to see the skills modeled, be reminded of the skills, and held accountable for the use of the skills. Second, at the youngest grade levels, whether we like to admit it or not, social skills to a very large extent, *are* the curriculum. If, in the youngest grades, students learn to support and encourage each other, listen carefully to the ideas of others, and work quietly and efficiently in groups, then they have received instruction predictive of future academic and life success. Grades K-2 lay the foundation for the entire schooling experience. By stressing social skills at the earliest grades we provide the positive social context among students which will lead to school success. If each student is motivated and knows how to help each other student, all classrooms will have thirty teachers instead of one.

As I look at some of the methods Lorna uses to emphasize social skills, I take some pause. For example, my instincts do not incline toward having students do finger evaluations on social skills. If we think about it, though, by a heavy emphasis on evaluation of the skills Lorna keeps the focus on the skills and holds the students accountable for the use of the skills. Evaluation produces meta-cognitive awareness as the students look back on what skills they are using.

Management for K-2
Lorna's detailed description of management techniques for the K-2 classroom is a major contribution to Cooperative Learning. Management tips together with those for Social Skills, are what was missing for so long in providing teachers with the resources necessary for success with Cooperative Learning for the youngest pupils.

New Structures for K-2
Those teachers familiar with my work in the structural approach to cooperative learning will find in this book some new structures and adaptations of old ones for K-2 classrooms. Lorna begins her classroom with Community Circle. When I first looked at this structure I thought it was traditional, whole-class instruction in disguise. Only one person at a time is talking, and the person is talking to the whole class. There is a very critical difference, however, between Community Circle and Whole-Class: The students are all oriented toward each other. Lorna uses the structure as a first step in moving the little ones away from an orientation toward the teacher, to an orientation toward each other. As soon as they learn the norms and standards necessary to listen to each other, Lorna begins to have more than one circle, allowing simultaneous interaction and a progression toward Cooperative Learning.

Lorna contributed to the 1989 Summer Training Institutes in the Structural Approach. Her K-2 breakout sessions were extremely popular. Numerous teachers have reported back success with Happy Talk, Community Circle, and Active Listening — original contributions by Lorna.

Some of her variations on structures were born from the management requirements necessary for K-2 classrooms, but will become useful at all grade levels. For example, the split class Line-Up is a very elegant solution to the problem of efficiently getting everyone in the class talking with another student with a very different point of view. Some of the adaptations are pure K-2, like the yarn or tape used for Line-Ups and the Roundtable Sequencing Board. Notice, that Similarity Grouping does not occur — rather Lorna uses Corners only. Why? Similarity Grouping, in the K-2 classroom can be a management nightmare, whereas Corners is a dream.

Lorna is to be complimented also for some better terms for some of what we do in Cooperative Learning. "Reflection Time" is so much more descriptive than "Processing." "Spilt and Slide" says it far better than "a Split Value Line," just as "The Wrap" is far more descriptive for little ones that calling it a "Folded Value Line."

I must admit that Lorna has left out a few of my favorite structures. Teachers will not find in the book a Three-Step Interview, Carousel, or Leap-Frog Jigsaw. But Cooperative Learning is so big that no one book can cover it all, and what is provided is so extensive we can hardly fault Lorna for not working every structure into her lessons. The book was not generated with an eye toward giving examples of all possibilities.

The process was far more organic. Lorna had been doing Cooperative Learning successfully for some time before she received training from me in the structural approach. She began incorporating structures into her lessons, but main-tained many other methods which had proved successful. Thus the book is somewhat eclectic -- and far richer than one which would come from any single approach.

Literature-Based Lessons

Literature is a natural springboard for Cooperative Learning. Good literature motivates communication, and is per-haps the best entry point for K-2 Cooperative Learning. Lorna is to be complimented on the rich assortment of literature she provides and for integrat-ing her lessons. Although the lessons have been categorized into sections, the categories are necessarily somewhat arbi-trary. Consistent with the new Language Arts framework, the lessons are integrat-ed so that most lessons contain reading, writing, listening, and speaking.

More than a Set of Lessons

Although the book provides well-tested, successful lessons which will allow any K-2 teacher to easily begin Cooperative Learning, what Lorna and I both hope is that teachers do not just come away from the book with thirty six lessons to try. Rather, the book provides a philosophy of teaching and an approach to Cooperative Learning for little ones which can be used with any content.

Spencer Kagan, Ph.D.
December 1989

Acknowledgements

by Lorna Curran

I would like to give thanks to those who have helped me gain knowledge, those who have provided ideas, and those who have given me the encouragement and support necessary to complete this book. Jim Wray, Judy De Wolf, Corine Madrid and Gene Hawley worked side by side with me helping me to gain knowledge by sharing everything they knew about cooperative learning with me. They also modeled for me effective techniques for teaching teachers about cooperative learning.

I owe thanks to ABC School District personnel for providing opportunities for me to learn more about cooperative learning from David and Roger Johnson, Dee Dishon and Pat Wilson O'Leary, and Spencer Kagan.

The teachers at Aloha Elementary School provided me with classrooms at all grade levels where I could experiment with the knowledge I had gained from the cooperative learning experts. A special thanks to several of the Aloha teachers. Cathy Green and I started using cooperative learning at about the same time. Having classrooms next to each other, we had the perfect opportunity to peer coach each other through successful lessons and lessons that needed quite a bit of revision to work smoothly and accomplish the goals we had intended. Pattie Mancillas has been a valuable resource by finding books I have needed for cooperative learning lessons in her vast collection of children's literature books. She often shares new books that she feels I could use to create a new cooperative learning lesson. My current teaching partner in kindergarten, Jean Chee, deserves thanks also for being understanding when I wanted to try a new cooperative learning structure or when I wanted to change traditional independent lessons into cooperative learning projects to see how it would affect the students' interest and learning. Because we plan our kindergarten program together, most often she was caught up in my enthusiasm for the cooperative approach to a lesson and agreed to that format even though the original plans were for an independent activity.

Also, I owe a great deal to Spencer Kagan, who has taught me so much about the variety of cooperative learning structures that are available to use across the curricular areas. I thank him for permission to use parts of his definitions of the cooperative learning structures from his book *Cooperative Learning*, and for suggesting and helping with numerous revisions of both the structure and content of the book. It was his constant prodding that finally got me to flesh out my lesson ideas into the present printed form. With his guidance, the original lesson outlines have become fully explained, easy to follow lessons.

At various stages in this project the following staff members from *Kagan Cooperative Learning* have made valuable contributions: Bill Rutherford, Miguel Kagan, Simon Kagan, Chris Broders, Benjamin Taylor, Jason Lucente, and Catherine Hurlbert. Celso Rodriguez produced much of the delightful art. Many thanks to Pat Lederer who was a primary contact with the staff.

Thanks to Jeanne Stone for suggestions on Language Arts materials. A special thanks to Paula Lee, a first grade student at Aloha Elementary School in the ABC School District for her contribution of art for the cover.

A loving thanks to my husband, Tim, who has spent many hours by himself while I composed and then pounded away at my typewriter. I owe him many hours of togetherness.

Lorna Curran

Lorna Curran
December 1989

Preface

As a mentor teacher with a focus on cooperative learning, I was continually asked to teach teachers of all grade levels many different cooperative learning structures and to model these structures in their classrooms. Each time I would model a structure in a classroom, I wanted to incorporate lessons that would enrich the topics the class was studying. Soon I had a collection of lessons using many of the structures which were mostly for third through sixth grade classes. Teachers would often say, "Put those lessons together into a book."

Then I was asked to teach kindergarten. I went looking for help. I went to cooperative learning conferences seeking information to help me work with the young students. I found instead that I would come back with many wonderful ideas to use with upper grade students. I wasn't alone. There were many primary teachers out there asking what to do. All of us were correctly told that most cooperative learning lessons could be used across the grade levels. All we needed to do was to adapt the lessons to our grade level. But it takes time to adapt these upper grade lessons and adjust the format of lessons so they could be handled by much younger students.

Unless the presenter has had experience teaching young students, it is hard for her to suggest organizational tips and management techniques that help young students transition from one part of the lesson to the next; ideas that make the lesson flow smoothly from beginning to end.

I was convinced that cooperative learning made for a more positive feeling tone because the students receive positive feedback from everyone in class, rather than just from me. I liked that the students took responsibility for their own behavior as well as for their academic work. I didn't want to become the sole disciplinarian again. So I began to explore ways to use the same cooperative learning standards and lesson structure for younger students.

I suddenly needed to revise my collection of lessons so they could be done by students who could do little or no writing, children who lacked the wealth of background information that older students have acquired, and students who have shorter attention spans. The younger students needed more structure, more variety of activities, and more frequent praise and rewards. They also needed a lot of guidance in knowing how to share ideas, ask for help, give suggestions, and give praise.

So now I have a large collection of lessons for those structures I have found appropriate for kindergarten, first grade, and second grade students. These include Roundtable, Line-ups, Corners, Formations, Partners, and Cooperative Projects. This time I did heed my friends' advice. In order to make this book, I started putting together the lessons that kindergarten, first and second grade students have enjoyed. I also started collecting management tips and hints to make the lessons a rewarding experience for both students and teachers.

I hope that by trying some of the lessons in this book, you and your class will become hooked on cooperative learning and will want to use a variety of cooperative learning structures to enhance a variety of topics. By looking at the suggestions as to how to apply the lesson structures to various topics, you will soon be creating your own lessons that are tailored specifically to the wants and needs of you and your students.

Overview

The book starts out with a general overview of using cooperative learning in the primary grades. Chapter 1 concludes with an explanation of the lesson format which was designed to make implementation of cooperative learning easy and enjoyable for all teachers and their students. It continues by addressing some of the advantages of using cooperative learning to strengthen the students' ability to use oral and written language. Next is a look at the value of connecting the lessons to children's favorite pieces of literature.

Chapter 2 provides suggestions for forming groups: group size and group composition. It provides information on introducing, reinforcing and maintaining the social skills. Information on effective lesson facilitation is included along with ideas for assisting students who need help developing positive social skills.

Chapter 3 explains the importance of each Social Skill and provides suggestions on how to incorporate the Social Skills within the lesson. The structures used in the lessons are presented in alphabetical order in Chapter 4. Each structure is defined so that the information is specific to using that structure with young students.

The rest of the book contains lessons based on well-known children's literature. These cooperative learning lessons develop the student's understanding or appreciation of some aspect of the story that has been read to them or read by them. These lessons are organized into sections that address sharing ideas, establishing values, developing oral language, learning about letters, and developing reading and writing skills.

The Table of Contents indicates the main language arts skill associated with each lesson, although most of the lessons have integrated reading, writing, listening and speaking. Following the Table of Contents is the Table of Structures which indicates which lessons contain each structure. The Table of Social Skills follows, indicating which lessons contains specific social skills. Thus a teacher interested in using a specific structure or social skill, can easily find lessons to use or adapt. The main literature book upon which each lesson is based is listed in the materials box of each lesson. Other books that could be used with the lessons are mentioned in the Background Information section or in the Other Applications section of each lesson. A bibliography is included at the back of the book to facilitate reserving the books at the library, or purchasing the book.

Suggestions specific to each lesson, are included in many of the lessons to help the teacher with procedural options, or to provide rationale for the procedures that are incorporated in the lessons. Actual dialogue provides suggestions as to how to word the directions for the students. Sample student responses are often given so you can anticipate the type of answers students may give.

Connection to Spencer Kagan's *Cooperative Learning*

The lessons included in this book incorporate structures I learned while receiving cooperative learning training from Spencer Kagan. While practicing the structures I began to write and use some of these lessons with my students. This book gives sample lessons for his Cooperative Learning structures that I found to be effective with young students. My description of the structures provides information specific to primary teachers. For further information on each structure, and other structures that you might find effective for your students, I refer you to Spencer Kagan's book *Cooperative Learning*. His book will provide in-depth information on rationale for using certain structures, procedure for using the structures, and ideas of how to apply each structure in a variety of content areas.

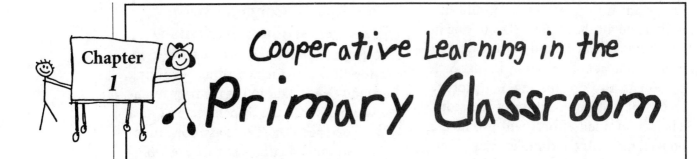

A Picture of Primary Cooperative Learning

The room is humming with excitement. Students are leaning in, almost nose to nose. Everyone is anxious to hear what is said and have a chance to contribute their own ideas. As you listen, you hear pairs of students contributing many ideas about places where they could go in their shoes. You hear other pairs deciding which place would be the best for the two of them. Still other partners are sharing their papers to draw a picture that shows the two of them in the new place. But hear something that is even more wonderful than that. "Terrific idea!" "You made a great tree." "You're doing a great job on that building." These are some of the warm and wonderful comments that are being shared in the groups as they work. You look again at the students in the class and realize these are very small sized students who are doing large sized jobs like gathering ideas, coming to consensus on which ideas to use for their team project, and complimenting and encouraging each other as they work. These kindergarten students are working together as well as any adult group would as they solve problems in group situations.

Primary students can be very successful with cooperative learning. The emphasis on social skills, along with the structure of the lesson, teaches all students the things they need to say and do to work well together. By focusing on one social skill at a time, students find that learning how to work together becomes an enjoyable experience.

The Need for Cooperative Learning in Language Arts

Students of all ages need to have many opportunities to listen to language and then to practice using language orally. But young students especially need many opportunities to listen and speak so they will develop good communication skills and become familiar with the vocabulary and syntax of language. As students share ideas in groups, they will increase their vocabularies, learning from each other synonyms for objects, feelings and events. Children who have had little experience using language and those who are learning to use a new language will hear the patterns and rhythm of language as they listen to and participate in groups discussions. Developing this familiarity with language will help make it easy for all students to become fluent readers and writers.

Kindergarten students use the illustrations in books to retell stories, they will also use pictures to help them remember important information they would like to share about the stories. By working in groups, they can record a great deal of information about a story by having each person in the groups make a picture record of just one portion of the story. Their combined efforts will produce a booklet that tells the complete story. Few kindergarten children would have the time and patience to record the whole story, but by working together they are successful.

As students learn to read, they can become experts who assist each other in remembering the vocabulary of the stories they want to read. They feel comfortable helping each other remember words and ideas from the stories. They enjoy taking turns reading in groups so they have a small audience to hear them read and they only have a short wait to get their turn to read.

As students go through the stages of the writing process, group work can result in better quality writing. In the prewriting stage they can gather many more ideas if they brainstorm and cluster ideas with other students. In the writing stage, it builds the students self confidence if they can do a practice writing with a group before they have to do an independent writing assignments. Also many students like to have a writing partner or group who they can turn to for advice while they are writing. Revision is easier when the student is comfortable working with her partner or group . Members of this group with can share what is best about the writing and also can tell what things would make the writing even better.

The Need for Cooperative Learning for Young Students

Young students are very egocentric. They think of the world as revolving around them. Our job as primary teachers is to broaden the "I" perspective into a "We" perspective. The classroom functions so much better when we are working together as a unit or family. Cooperative learning helps the students focus on one social skills at a time. This makes caring about and working with others a manageable and enjoyable task.

Another difference in primary students is that they can not read and write fluently. The lessons in the book are built around activities that can be done orally, with pictures or with few written words.

Managing Cooperative Learning for Young Students

The lessons also include special management tips that help young students be successful. There are suggestions for developing comprehensible directions, for modeling the lesson, deciding on group size, for developing the social skills, and for using praise and rewards to increase use of social skills. There ideas on how to form teams and how long teams should stay together.

There are many signals that students and teachers can give during cooperative learning lessons that help the lessons flow smoothly with minimal interruptions. There are suggestions for interruptions that can focus students on the social skills and increase the learning they acquire from the lesson.

Finally there are ideas on how to help those students who have a difficult time working with others. Ideas on how to help them acquire the necessary social skills. Ideas on what to do when they can't use the social skill. Ideas on how the teams can help these students.

Use of Literature

The lessons in this book capture the students interest because they are based on ideas of characters from stories they love. The students enjoy doing lessons that hone their listening, speaking, reading and writing skills, when the materials they are working with are about their favorite story characters. They think they are just doing a fun game or activity about a favorite story.

Using ideas from literature also helps the students make connections with other content areas. *Reliving Repunzel, A Good Friend For Me,* and *Beary Good and Beary Bad* connect to social studies by having the students discuss values as they try to decide if ideas and actions in the stories are appropriate or inappropriate. *Favorite Farm Fauna, Colorful Chameleons,* and *Talking Trees* are lessons that add interest and motivation to science lessons.

Lesson Format Makes Cooperative Learning Easy

The lessons in this book are easy for students because the lessons provide the students with an overview of the lesson and then break the lesson down into short, easy-to-understand sections. The students are also provided with samples of what to say and do.

The lessons make cooperative learning easy for the teacher because everything the students need to do is listed, stem-by-step, in the lessons. Much of the dialogue the teacher can use with the students is also included. A box, Curran's Comments, provides rationale or suggestions that apply to that lesson.

Suggestions on how to extend the lessons or do more lessons using the same unit or theme are included in some lessons. Variations tell how to adapt the lessons to different grade or ability levels. Some of the variations refer to use of different materials.

Organizing & Managing Cooperative Learning

This chapter provides information on how to plan cooperative learning lessons to assure they will be successful and enjoyable for both students and teacher. It gives management tips that will help the lesson run smoothly from beginning to end. First are suggestions on using different sized groups for cooperative learning and some suggestions of structures that work well for each size group. Next is a description of the three cooperative learning standards that need to be in place so the students feel they have a safe, risk-free environment in which to work. The next section includes a description of all the components of a cooperative learning lesson. A section on use of praise and rewards gives suggestions on how group members can give each other special recognition or how the whole class can be rewarded for completing the task and using the social skills. A list of signals and commands that can help the lessons flow smoothly are included in the next section.

This chapter ends with additional teaching tips that answer questions teachers often ask.

✖ How can you make sure all group members participate?

Answer: Make sure the students in the group are really interdependent and really need each other. Types of interdependence are listed and described.

✖ How do group members know what tasks to do so all do a fair share?

Answer: Think through the lesson, note all jobs to be done, choose the best way for your students to find out their responsibilities. Suggestions for beginning and more advanced students are given.

✖ What is the best way to form teams?

Answer: Seeing primary students seldom know the criteria for forming well balanced teams, the teacher should form the teams. If the teams are meeting for a short term activity the teams could be formed by random selection. Tips provided for both type of team selection.

✖ What do you do with the students who have a difficult time working with other students?

Answer: Check the team formation, provide composure time, have conferences with students and/or parents about social skills, and promote team support for persons needing help. Suggestions for using these remediation techniques are described.

Progression of Group Size

Each teacher will introduce new groupings, practice them until the students feel comfortable using them, and then move on to new groupings that fit the needs of the students and the content and type of lessons that are being taught. I will share the progression of groupings I generally use. These can be used as a general guide for how you might like to progress with your students.

Whole Class

Whole class structures are used at the beginning of the year so the students in the class can learn information about each other. As they learn about each other, their names, facts about their lives, or their likes and dislikes, it becomes easier for them to really care about each other as they work together. Several of the cooperative learning structures such as Community Circle, Corners, and Line Up, are especially useful for helping students learn about each other. Community Circle (see Chapter 4) is the structure I start with because students learn something about each other and at the same time they are provided with excellent opportunities to practice active listening. Active listening in my opinion, is the most important of the cooperative learning standards. Until students know how to be good active listeners, it is difficult for them to work effectively together in cooperative activities. Community Circle also makes the students aware of the necessity for being good speakers.

Corners and Line-Ups are two more structures that help the students learn about each other as the students group themselves either in corner groups or along a line according to facts about

themselves or their feelings about a certain issue. Students feel comfortable as they have a chance to talk along the Line-Up first with students with similar interests and feelings, and then they become very curious as they do two variations of the Line-Up, The Split and Slide or The Wrap, to talk to students who have experienced different situations or have different ideas and feelings.

Pairs

Partners is the next grouping I use because it is easiest for the students to work with just one other person when they are deciding on an answer to a question, or agreeing on and producing a product.

During discussions, partners are always involved as either listeners or speakers. Turns come frequently and there is minimal wait time. Materials need to be shared with only one other person. That there are only two people, also is the weakness of Partners. If there are students who have poorly developed social skills, they need to be placed with the most caring students in class. However, in fairness to these caring students, the partnerships should be rotated quite frequently so they don't always have to put forth that extra effort of working with students who have exceptional social needs.

Triads

The next group size I usually use is Triads. This configuration is used for group projects that have three parts and each team member is responsible for completing a part, such as, reporting on the beginning, middle, and end of a story.

When students work in triads, they have to wait a little longer. During discussions, they may have to wait for two other students to speak before they can speak, but more ideas are generated. There are more students to share the equipment but there are also more hands to complete the job. Having tasks assigned by either the students or the teacher becomes important so everyone knows who is accountable for each portion of the team project.

Groups of Four

Groups of four are generally used after the students have had successful experiences with pairs and triads. Groups of four are useful for large group projects in which there are four parts to be completed, or where it is important to gather many ideas, such as in Sequential or Simultaneous Roundtable. Groups of four also can be used as sharing groups for two pairs to share their answers or products with each other.

Groups of 5 or 6

Groups of this size are usually used in the primary grades for group projects that have five distinct sections or topics. Each person agrees to do a section. Then all sections are combined into a group product. A story may have five characters and each group member draws or writes about an incident, a point of view, or a quote from that particular character. If there were six characters, I might move to groups of six.

Simplifying Cooperative Learning Standards

Standards

There are three social skills which are so central to the primary classroom that I call them Standards. To crea[...] ronment for cooperative le[...] dents learn the standard[...] Listening, Happy Talk, and Everyo[...] Participates. Consistent use of these Standards provides a comfortable, positive atmosphere, in which students are willing to share ideas and work together.

Primary teachers find it is easy for students to remember the cooperative learning standards if they are written in simple phrases and include pictures to help convey the message. In the primary classroom the standards could be written as they are in the box on the next page.

Active Listening

The most important of the cooperative learning standards, and the one to teach the students first, is Active Listening. Until the class is really ready to listen to the students as they speak, they will not be very willing to share their ideas. The class needs to show they are interested in listening by looking at the speaker, listening to what they say, and by keeping distracting objects put away.

As the chart is presented to the students they are given the following definition for each of the symbols. "The eyes remind you to look at the person who is supposed to be speaking. The ears remind you to listen to the words that are said and think about what they mean. The hands remind you to keep you hands in your lap (or on your desk) so they won't bother you or anybody else."

Happy Talk

Happy Talk involves development of a repertoire of positive statements that students say to each other as they work together. Use of these statements is called

Happy Talk because it recognizes the positive contributions each individual makes toward the team effort. Sample Happy Talk statements from my kindergarten class are included on the standards chart. Your class could compose and post their own statements which are appropriate for their team projects.

Everyone Participates

This standard makes it so everyone is willing to work hard for the team because they know that everyone will be responsible for completing their fair share. The tasks necessary to complete the project are identified and then assigned in various ways. The trick is to have the tasks assigned in such a way that the students feel they have been fairly distributed. Then the teams start their work in a positive way.

As the students first start doing the cooperative lesson, it seems to work best to have the tasks assigned. The fairest and easiest way to assign tasks is for the students to number themselves with in the team and then either use oral directions (as in the lesson Help Me With ABC) or a chart to describe the tasks for each number (see the lesson Sense-a-tional Stories). The students do the task that matches their number.

Standards

Active Listening
Look at the speaker.
Listen to what is said.
Have your hands in your lap.

Happy Talk
I like your coloring.
Nice job.
Pretty Coloring.
Super duper job.
I like how you stay in the lines.
That's a very good job.

Everyone Participates
Right to pass.

A similar way of assigning tasks is to have a colored card as a task designator for each team member. After the cards have been selected by the team members, a color coded chart is displayed which lists the tasks to be completed.

To keep the assignment of tasks fair, the students need to select their task designator card before they know which tasks are associated with that card. If they know what each number or color stands for, they could argue about who would have which task designator card.

Or each team member can reach into an envelope that contains all the tasks. With out looking, each person reaches in the envelope and takes out a slip of paper, signs that slip of paper and does that task for the team (See the lesson Retell Rosie).

When they are used to sharing the jobs, they then are ready to make team decisions on who should do each of the tasks. When those decisions are made, they sign up for their task on the team task sheet. Everyone then knows who is responsible for each of the jobs on the team. This is especially important when each person has more that one job to do for the team. Also observers can tell if everyone is on target.

For some cooperative lessons, everyone just pitches in to complete the job. There are no distinct jobs, so everyone pitches in and completes the job and then signs the product to show that they contributed to the completion of the job and agree with the final product.

Components of a Cooperative Learning Lesson

Two Objectives

All cooperative learning lessons have two objectives, the cognitive objective and the social skills objective. To keep the students from having to focus on too many things at once in a lesson, we make sure that only one of the objectives is new or difficult for the students. If the cognitive objective is covering new materials, the social skill objective is one the students know very well. If the social skill is new or one that is still difficult for the students, then the cognitive objective covers material that is easy for the students to handle.

Instruction/Review of the Social Skill

Before the students do the cooperative lesson, they need to think about how they can use the social skill effectively. The teacher could make a chart that lists their ideas on how to use the social skill. This is what Spencer Kagan calls the "gambits." Making "Does" and "Says" Charts helps them know how to act and what to say as they use the social skill. The Happy Talk statements on the sample Standards Chart are examples of gambits. The gambit chart can be used as the criteria for their evaluation of the social skill at the end of the lesson. These "gambit" charts can be made either before or after the lesson is modeled for the students.

Clear Directions

Primary students need lessons that are explained with clear, step-by-step directions they can follow from the beginning to the end of the lesson. It helps if the directions are given in a written, as well as an oral form. The wording of the directions needs to be simple enough so the students will be able to read and understand them. Often as groups are working, I see them pause a minute, read the direction chart just to be sure they are doing the activity correctly, and then proceed through the lesson. Directions written for kindergarten and first grade students should contain a few simple words for each step of the procedure accompanied by pictures that illustrate the directions for them. See the sample direction chart on the next page.

The teacher reads the words written on the chart, but for the kindergarten student it is the pictorial clues that help them as they work their way through the lesson. First grade students begin to focus more on the written part of the directions.

For students at the end of first grade and beyond, charts can be completely written, but they still should be written in short easy phrases and sentences. To help students at this level understand which tasks they are responsible for, the charts can be color coded. Before the directions are read, each team is given a pack of colored cards.

A Place for Partners

Talk about places to go.

Both draw the picture.

Use Happy Talk.

Practice sharing :

  One holds.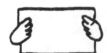

  One talks.

In the pack are enough cards so each team member will be able to select a different colored card. If there are four members on each team, there would be four different colors in each pack. Directions for all of them to follow, would be written on white paper. Any job that is for a specific team member, would be written on paper that is the same color as one of the colored cards that a member of each team is holding.

Third grade students should be able to follow directions without pictures or color coding. It helps though at all grade levels to keep the wording and or picture symbols as consistent as possible from lesson to lesson.

Modeling Lessons

All students remember a procedure better if they have a chance to see it before they need to do it themselves. This is especially true for the primary students, who find it more difficult than older students to follow written directions. The teacher can model the lesson or students can be part of a demonstration team to model the lesson. If it is a short, easy activity, the students remember it well by watching the teacher's demonstration. If the activity is more involved, the students remember better by watching a team made up of their teacher and peers, go through a sample activity.

Another advantage of having students involved in the demonstration is that the students who were involved in the demonstration have gotten extra practice and are now experts in how to do that particular lesson. Often, I will ask students who I feel might have some difficulty doing the lesson to be part of the demonstration lesson. This extra practice

with me as part of the demonstration team, gives them extra self confidence before they do the activity with their team.

Another reason I like to have students help me demonstrate the lesson, is that as a member of a demonstration team, I can help model the social skill for that lesson. If the social skill is using Happy Talk, I use a lot of Happy Talk statements while our team works, such as: "That is a good idea." "I like your coloring." "What a terrific house you made." If the social skill were to do paraphrasing, I would be sure to restate what had been said in different words. Because I start doing the social skill, the team usually starts to do it too. Then the class sees and hears examples of what the social skill looks and sounds like.

If the class has already brainstormed a list of phrases to use while they work together, they have an idea of how to use those phrases as they progress through the lesson. If the lesson is demonstrated before the chart is made, having seen the lesson and having heard the demonstration team's comments, the class has a better idea of what kind of statements to suggest. No matter what the social skill, seeing the teacher and the demonstration students, helps show behaviors that develop positive interaction within the teams.

The Cooperative Lesson or Activity

While the students are engaged in the cooperative lesson or activity, the teacher has several responsibilities. These responsibilities are:

Be a facilitator and...

... have procedure charts on display so the students will be able to remember what tasks need to be done.

... have gambit charts on display so the students can get help on what to say and do as they use the social skills.

... set time limits so teams know how long they have to complete the tasks.

... insert sponge activities so teams will have constructive activities to do when they finish.

... direct the evaluation, validation, debriefing, and sharing.

Observe, take notes, and..

... watch for effective use of social skills.

... notice individual strengths that can be used when forming new groups.

... look for any improvements that can be made in the lesson design or directions.

... notice any difficulties in social interactions, these can be the social skills to focus on for the next few lessons.

Praise and...

... give signals or verbal praise to groups who are using the social skills.

... give points or rewards to groups who are following the procedure and social skills.

Give Guidance by...

... answering team questions if all team members have their hands raised.

... frequently visiting groups where students have a potential for having difficulties.

... helping groups find solutions to their problems by having them review what they have already done and think of other things they could do.

... leading groups on to the next step of the procedure.

Evaluation Techniques
A. When To Evaluate
Students often need to be reminded of the social skill several times during the lesson. There are three times during the lesson where it is common to focus on the social skills:

Before the lesson starts. After a demonstration team, made up of the teacher and some students, models how to do the lesson, students discuss what they saw and heard that were examples of the social skill being used in the lesson.

During the lesson. The teacher can stop the lesson to focus on the social skill for several reasons...

... To compliment and/or reward teams for using the social skill.

... To review with the students what the social skill looks and sounds like if the social skills haven't been used yet.

... To add variety to the gambits (positive phrases) the students are using.

After the lesson. Time should be taken at the end of a lesson to have students reflect on what they said and did to use the social skill and to decide what else they could have said or done to use the social skill.

B. How To Evaluate
It helps the students have an easy time with the evaluation if they know at the beginning of the lesson how they will be evaluating the social skill. Then as the lesson progresses they will remember specific information they want to share

during the evaluation. These following tips help make the evaluation positive and meaningful.

Introduce Evaluation. Explain the method of reporting the evaluation. The reporting methods are given in an order of difficulty from easiest to hardest, so it is advisable to start with the easier types of evaluation at the top of the list. Then progress to the more difficult types when the students have some experience with cooperative learning.

Types of Signals.
Signs
* Thumb signals
  * thumbs up = we did it
  * thumbs sideways = we need to fix it
* Finger signals
  * five fingers = we all did the social skill
  * three fingers = most of us did the social skills
  * one finger = we tried but need more practice

Oral Statements
* Oral statements ("You made it easy for me today by.....")

Written Feedback
* Written symbol (happy face or star)
* Written number which can be done by counting up the finger signals
* Written comment about what worked best and what could be better next time

Reflection Time. Give the students reflection time to remember how the team used the social skill.

Student Evaluations. Call on students to give their evaluation and validate (give reasons) for the evaluation.

Generalize. Use the words someone, somebody, or some or us, instead of names during the validation.

Rewards. Teams can receive praise or certificates for use of the social skill. See sample rewards.

Debriefing
A. Reasons for Debriefing
At the completion of every new type of cooperative learning lesson, or after the introduction of a new social skill, the students should have a chance to let you know how they felt about doing the lesson. It is a great feeling at the end of a successful lesson to discuss the factors that made it turn out so well.

It is also important to find out if there were some things that some of the team members didn't feel comfortable about. Even in an excellent lesson, there may be a couple of features that could be altered to improve the lesson. There also could have been a couple of personal interactions that could have been smoother.

Especially if a lesson didn't turn out as well as expected, it is a good idea to find out from the students which part of the lesson worked well and which parts could be changed to make the lesson easier, more enjoyable, or more understandable.

The debriefing should ask questions that cover all parts of the lesson; the planning, the preparation, the assembling of the product, the practice for the presentation, and the presentation itself. Also, questions need to be asked about the interactions between individuals as they used the social skill and evaluated its use at the end of the lesson.

B. Types of Debriefing

At the end of the lesson, time should be provided for the students to analyze how they felt about the lesson. The teacher can have a class discussion and call on some students to find out how each of those persons felt about the lesson. Or the teacher can have team discussions to find out how the team members felt about the content, the structure and the interactions.

1. Total Class Debriefing

A class discussion can be used to do the debriefing. Usually, in this case, just a few of the students share their ideas. If the students do a Think-Pair-Share to discuss and share the debriefing questions, then all the students have a chance to discuss ideas with each other even though only a few of the students may share the ideas with the whole class. The following are a sampling of the questions that can be used when debriefing is done with a class discussion.

- What made this easy/difficult for you?
- How did it feel when it was your turn to share? Explain.
- How did it feel while it was your turn? Explain.
- How did it feel when the group used Happy Talk? Explain.
- How did it feel when you used Happy Talk? Explain.
- For you, what was the best thing about this lesson? Why?

- What would make a lesson like this better for you next time?

2. Team Debriefing

By having a team discussion for the debriefing, everyone has a chance to participate in the discussion. Everyone becomes more involved in the analysis of the procedures and interactions that occurred in the lesson. Everyone has more interest in planning improvements for the next time the teams work together. These are a few questions that could be used for a debriefing that uses team discussion.

- What did the team do best today? Why did it turn out so well?
- What did the team do that made the job easy?
- What did your team do that helped you?
- Why was this easier to do as a team than to do alone?
- What could the team do to make it easier to do the job next time?

Sponge Activities

Not all teams work at the same rate. To assure that teams who finish the lesson more quickly are busy doing a meaningful activity, a sponge activity can be assigned. Teams know they are to automatically start the sponge activity when their lesson is complete. The sponge activity is a challenging, fun project usually closely related to the lesson just completed.

Signals and Commands

Teaching the students several commands and signals that trigger recall of specific directions, helps the lessons flow smoothly. By saying a few words or by giving various hand signals, students can change from one type of activity to another both quickly and quietly.

Active Listening Signal

The Active Listening signal is used to help primary students give full attention to a designated speaker. When the command "Show Active Listening!" is given, the students signal back by folding their hands together and looking at the speaker. The students are taught that Active Listening consists of the three following components:

Look. Use your eyes and look at the person who is supposed to be talking.

Listen. Use your ears to listen to and think about what the speaker is saying.

Quiet Hands. Fold your hands together so you know what they are doing and they won't bother you or anyone else.

Students can discuss these rules, to decide how those rules help them to be good listeners. It is easier for the primary students to remember the components of Active Listening if they are given visual representations for each one. Teachers have made charts with simple written directions using visual clues similar to those on the chart on the following page so the students can check to see that they are doing all parts of Active Listening when the command is given.

Finished Signal

A quick way to find out when teams have done their job is to ask them to give the Finished Signal when they have completed the lesson. To do the finished signal, all team members rest one hand or both hands on top their heads. This quickly and quietly gives you the message without bothering other teams or gives you a quiet answer from all teams if you are checking with the total class.

Silent Signal

The Silent Signal is used when the teams are doing any activity which involves a lot of discussion, and all the teams might not hear when the teacher ask for Active Listening. For the Silent Signal, the teacher puts up one hand with the index finger raised and says, "Show the Silent Signal, please." Students are to raise one hand, have the other hand empty, and look at the teacher. As soon as team members see the Silent Signal, they are to remind the other team members to give the signal by raising their hands too.

Combination Silent Signal and Active Listening

When students are using manipulatives, writing tools, or art supplies, they often give the silent signal with one hand and keep on working with the other hand. They will be quiet but they will still be concentrating on their work rather than listening. If the students are asked to give the silent signal and change it to active listening, the students then have their hands together and all their supplies are put down. They are now ready to concentrate on the message being given.

The Tap

When teams are deeply involved in a lesson or activity, it is sometimes difficult for them to see or hear the Active Listening or Silent Signal. The teacher, as facilitator of the cooperative learning activity, goes to those groups who have

Active Listening

Look!

Look at the speaker.

Listen!

Listen to what is said.

Quiet Hands!

Have your hands in
your lap.

Lorna Curran: *Lessons for Little Ones: Language Arts*©
Kagan Cooperative Learning • 1 (800) Wee Co-op

not seen or heard the signal. The teacher lightly touches the shoulder of one of the team members. This person then has the job of showing the rest of the team members which signal is being given, so they can all respond.

Ten Second Signal

To motivate the teams to give quick responses to the signals, the teacher can use the Ten Second Signal. To do the Ten Second Signal, the teacher gives a command such as "Show Active Listening" or "Silent Signal, please" and then, using a whisper, counts to ten, at the speed of about a count a second. If the teams all return the signal before the teacher reaches the count of ten, the class is praised and/or rewarded.

Speak Louder Signal

In order for the students to be active listeners, they must be able to hear what the speaker is saying. So the students need to learn an easy way to let the speakers know that they can't be heard. Anyone who is having a hard time hearing, simply raises a hand. If the speaker sees several hands raised, he/she knows he/she needs to start using a louder voice. By using the signal, the speaker isn't interrupted, yet knows how to modify his or her voice to accommodate the needs of the audience.

Team Question Signal

If a team member has a question, it is that member's responsibility to ask each of the team members if they have the necessary information before the teacher can be asked to help. This makes the the team members reliant on each other as a valuable source of information. If between them they cannot solve their problem, all team members raise their hands and that is a signal to the teacher that there is a real need for help.

Two Tiered Timing

The last piece of information that is given to the students, as part of their directions, is the amount of time the lesson should take. This helps even kindergarten students, who do not have well developed sense of time, have a general idea whether they will have a long or short amount of time to do the lesson. If the students are told the total amount of time they will have to complete the lesson, many teams will finish but some teams will not be done and have to turn in an incomplete project which can deflate the team's esteem. Other teams will work very quickly and have nothing constructive to do.

A solution to the problem is to use Two Tiered Timing. To use Two Tiered Timing, the teacher breaks the working time he/she would like the students to use, into two sections. The first section of time lets the students how much time the lesson might take. The second time stated lets the students know the maximum amount of time allotted for the lesson.

The directions for a 15 minute lesson would sound like this: "We might finish this lesson in 10 minutes, but we must finish in 15 minutes. I will give you the Silent Signal when 10 minutes is up to see if you are done." If Two Tiered Timing is used to tell them how much time they have, the teams work at their own pace during the first time period, taking as much time as they need to gather ideas and plan. They know they will still have the second period of time. The students are asked to give the Silent Signal and change it to Active Listening. They are asked to give the Finished Signal if their team is done.

During the second time period, teams that got the job done quickly, will be ready to find out about the sponge activity. Other teams that are almost done will be ready to start the sponge activity as soon as they finish the lesson. Teams that still had a lot to complete, will speed up so they can complete the job.

Additional Teaching Tips

Use of Lesson Components

All the components of a cooperative learning lesson should be used while the students are learning a new structure or when they are learning a new social skill. These necessary components are:

* Cognitive and social skills objectives.
* An overview or modeling of the lesson.
* Instruction on use of the social skills.
* Using the social skills while doing the lesson or activity.
* Evaluation of the social skill.
* Validation of the evaluation to find out the reasons for that particular evaluation.
* Debrief the lesson to find out how the students felt about the lesson.

There are reasons that a teacher might want to leave out a component of a cooperative learning lesson. One of the components that can be left out is the modeling of the lesson when students are familiar with the structure, the social skill, and the type of lesson or activity.

Evaluation of the social skill can be left out after it has been successfully used several times. Remember however that a social skill that isn't thought about for a while, tends to disappear. Debriefing a lesson isn't necessary after a structure has been used several times and everyone knows how they feel about using that structure.

Positive Interdependence

In a cooperative learning lesson, if all the students in the group really need each other to complete the project, they are truly interdependent. If the students don't need each other to complete the tasks, they will begin to work independently within the team and then the sharing of information and the development of social skills will not occur. Each cooperative learning lesson should contain one or more of these types of interdependence:

* All students work to make one product.
* The resources are limited.
* Each member is responsible for doing a specific portion of the lesson. A task sheet is signed so everyone knows who is responsible for each portion of the lesson.
* Tasks are assigned within the group where each team member can complete his/her task only if all previous tasks are done.
* Awards or praise are given only when there is evidence that all team members contributed to the product or used the social skills.
* Random selection is used when evaluating the team so the team needs to be sure that all members perform up to the criteria.

- A group progress chart is kept and the teams earn credit for products that are equal to or better that their previous work.
- Individual tasks can not be accepted from the team until all team members have their assignment complete.

Assigning Tasks

Tasks can either be assigned to group members, or they can choose what tasks they would like to do. For young students and students who are just starting to do cooperative learning, I like to have their tasks assigned so they won't argue about who will do which job. If they argue about their jobs, their group starts off with a bad feeling tone and this makes it difficult for them to work harmoniously together for the rest of the lesson. After teams are working well and the students understand that everyone must do their share for the team, then the team members can begin to assign jobs for their team. Tasks can be assigned in the following ways:

- Have a team member sign a task sheet. The person who signs for the job is responsible to complete it.
- Team members number themselves. Then the tasks are numbered. Each person does the task that has his/her number.
- Each team member draws a slip of paper out of an envelope which indicates his/her task.
- Teams assign tasks based on the talents or interests of their team members.

Forming Teams

When forming teams that will work together for several days or longer, I construct the teams carefully to help assure success. I make certain each team has someone who can be a leader and someone who could use some help developing their social skills. I also look at the talents so there will be a person who is comfortable doing each of these tasks: reader, writer, speaker, and illustrator. I try for equal numbers of girls and boys. Finally, I try to have students from different ethnic groups on each team so they can make their own unique contributions to the team.

If teams are meeting for just one activity, they could successfully be formed using random selection. Some methods of random selection are:

- Students with the same colored strips of paper form a team.
- Students who have the same shape are a team.
- Students match numbers and dots to form partners.
- Students match upper case and lower case letters to form partners.

Duration of Groups

Teachers often ask how long groups should stay together? The answer is there is no definite period of time that is best for groups to work together. Groups can work together for just one activity. They can be together for several days, several weeks or for most of the year.

At the beginning of the year I construct different groups for each activity so I have a chance to observe a variety of student interactions. As the year progresses I want groups to remain together for longer periods of time. At this point, they become a team that concentrates on strategies that enable them to do their best work and on procedures that help them improve their social skills as they work through the lessons.

There are several factors that determine how long groups work together:

- The type of activity being done. If it is a difficult task they could need several days to complete the job.
- The content being covered could determine how long groups meet together. An example would be groups who are writing math problems and sending them on to other groups to be solved. They might need to meet several times to develop the problems, make an answer key, solve other groups problems, get their problems back to be checked, and then decide how to write better problems for another group to solve. And so the cycle continues. If they are making a pattern together, they might meet just once to make the pattern, or they may continue to meet together to see how many different types of patterns they can make.
- If several of the students have difficulty with their social skills, groups might be changed often so those students would have the advantage of learning from many different people and so all groups get a chance to experience students with different levels of social development.

A procedure that works well for determining how long groups should work together is this. Have the students do some inclusion lesson and observe their interactions. If the group interactions were difficult, form new groups, trying to get group members that are more compatible. When you have groups that function well together, those groups could be kept together for quite a while. Do what works best with the students, you, and the material that is being taught.

Assisting Teams

Sometimes students have questions while they are working. They will raise their hands as they have always done before and hope to get an answer from the teacher so they can continue their work. When they are working in groups, I want to make them depend upon each other and not on me, so I use some of the strategies listed below to make them seek help from each other instead of the teacher.

- All team members must have their hands raised before the teacher comes to help.
- Find out what the team has already done to solve the problem.
- If many teams have similar questions, stop the lesson and do some instruction or go through the directions again.
- Have an observer from the team go to visit other teams to see how they are solving the problem.
- Have the teams share their successful strategies for problem solving so teams can learn problem solving techniques from each other.

Assisting Students with Special Needs Using Social Skills

One of the most frequent questions asked during workshops and conferences is, "What do you do with the students who have a hard time working with groups ?" This question refers to student with various problems that interfere with other students in the groups. Following are some of these problems a some suggested solutions.

Domination of Conversation: Talking Chips

There are some students who want to control the conversation when teams are planning together. A solution is to use Talking Chips. When using Talking Chips, each student in the group is given an equal number of tokens (I use construction paper circles that say "Talking Chips"). Each time a team member makes a contribution to the conversation, that person must put one of his/her talking chips on a pile in the center of the group. When a person has used all his/her talking chips, that person may not talk again until all team members have used all their talking chips. This assures equal access to the conversation by all team members.

Domination or Avoidance of the Activity: Task Sheets

Some students want to try to do the whole activity for the group; other students would like to take a free ride. If either of these happens then real cooperation is not happening. Students who are pushed out of the planning and constructing of the group activity feel useless, frustrated, or bored. Students who are left with the bulk of the work to do,

feel put upon and upset that the group gets credit when one person had to do most of the work. If, before they start working, the students sign up for the same number of jobs on team task sheets, which list all the tasks needed to complete the activity , then all team members will be responsible for an equal amount of the work. Also they can remember during the project just who is to do which job. It makes it easier for the team to facilitate the lesson because a quick look at the task sheet lets the teacher know if everyone is focused on their particular part of the lesson.

Disruptive Behavior: Several Suggestions

A student with disruptive behavior makes it very difficult for a team to complete their job. One portion of the job is not getting done and the others may be distracted as they try to do their parts of the team project. More that one disruptive student on a team makes it almost impossible for the team to function.

1. Teacher Formed Teams

As teams are formed, the teacher should make sure that there is no more than one student per team who has weak interpersonal skills. Also, there should be a student on each team who has well developed social skills and can be a role model for the other students on the team. Also, check personalities to assure that the students on the team can work well together.

2. Conference on Social Skills

For a student who is having difficulty using the social skills, that student can be taken aside before the cooperative lesson. Have a short discussion about the social skill for the upcoming lesson and what the student needs to work on to do well with that social skill. This sometimes helps these students be more successful with the social skills. Time spent with this student after the lesson helps to reinforce the things that worked well so they can be used again.

3. Change Groups

Sometimes just providing a different environment helps students have an easier time using the social skills. Try to put that student in a group that has very strong social skills and nurturing personalities.

4. Composure Time

If a student is having a difficult time using the social skills, it often helps if they have a time out so they can take time to gain control of their attitudes or emotions. It can just be a time out to start thinking about the correct behavior, or there can be an assignment waiting that needs to be done. However, these are the students who need the cooperative experience the most so they can develop their interpersonal skills. So allow them the opportunity to return to the group as soon as possible.

5. Conference and Contract

If the student continues to have a difficult time using the social skills, it is time to have a conference with the parent and child. Develop a contract that has the student focus on one aspect, like one particular social skill that he/she will work on for the next week. Parent, student and teacher sign the contract and decide on rewards and consequences that go with the contract. Meet weekly to discuss progress, rewards, and a new con-

tract that adds another social skill. It usually helps to have the student move to another group to start working on the contract. A new group may be found by:

- Asking a group with good social skills and nurturing personalities if they would work for a week with this student and help the student develop the social skill that is on the contract.
- Present the contract to the class and ask if there is a group who would work with the student with his/her contract.

Sponge Activities

Not all teams work at the same rate. To assure that teams who finish the lesson more quickly are busy doing a meaningful activity, a sponge activity can be assigned. Teams know they are to automatically start the sponge activity when their lesson is complete. The sponge activity is a challenging, fun project usually closely related to the lesson just completed. For example, if the team finishes the Place for Partners Picture, showing where they want to go, a sponge activity could be to draw on the back of the paper either the shoes they would wear, or a family member and something they would like to tell that family member about the place the partners went.

Use of Praise and Rewards

Part of what makes cooperative learning successful is the rewards the students receive for having done well with the social skill the lesson addresses. Just as students enjoy an excellent grade or a positive comment written on an assignment, when they have shown that they mastered the cognitive objective of a lesson, they also feel good if they are given praise or a tangible reward for having successfully demonstrated their ability to do the social skill. Rewards have the most effect if they are given immediately after the social skill has been performed. Also rewards given frequently when a social skill is first introduced helps students focus on that skill. They often actually over use it as they are first learning how to improve their interpersonal skills. Types of rewards that can be given are praise, points, certificates, and cumulative rewards.

Praise

Praise comes from the teacher, but also is given by students as they learn to use Happy Talk and Praising Statements. Students make Praising Statements as they work together to let each other know what they like about the work they are doing or what they like about how they are doing their work.

Points

Points may be given for teams who show evidence of following the social skill or for teams who have improved the amount or quality of their work because they used the social skill. Points can be given to individuals who encourage the rest of the team to do the social skill.

Rewards

There are many different types of rewards that can be given to team members or the team members can give to each other.

The Silent Cheer. All the team members can shake their hands in the air energetically to give the silent cheer which will not disturb other teams who still are working. Also the silent cheer can be given by the whole class without disturbing the class next door.

Round of Applause. All the team members can applaud, while moving their hands in a circular motion, to give the team members a round of applause for their effort in using the social skill.

Inside High Five. Once the students know what an Inside Voice is, they can start giving an Inside High Five to their team members. The Inside High Five is gentle so it makes no noise to disturb others and it causes no pain which is unpleasant and a distracting to all around.

Happy Face from the Group. The team has a discussion to recall how each team member used the social skill. When they remember what a team member did, a happy face is drawn on the group project by that person's name.

Praise and Encouraging Words from the Team. Team members think of praising statements to give each other to tell each person the things he/she did to help get the team job done.

Certificates and Awards. The team validates that they used the social skill by sharing with the class or with another group, the specific ways they used the social skill. Then either a certificate is given to the team as a whole and is fastened to their team product, or a certificate is given to each of the team members.

Extra Credit. Teams that use the social skill can earn extra credit either in points for the product or in points for the reward chart.

Cumulative Point Rewards

Cumulative points which are earned by teams, individuals, or the whole class can lead to a reward. When the class reaches a designated number of points, which they should be able to accomplish every two or three weeks, there is some special event for the class.

Primary students especially enjoy the following rewards:

- An extra recess on their playground.
- A recess on the older students playground.
- A popcorn or cookie party.
- Toys from home for a special play time.
- A free choice art time.
- A movie shown both forwards and backwards.

Certificates and Awards

Certificates and awards can be effective when a new social skill is introduced, or when the teams are having a difficult time using a particular social skill. The awards can be given to the team members by the teacher as she notices mastery of the particular social skill. The certificates also can be given to the team at the end of a lesson as both the team members and the teacher validate a team's use of the social skill by relating specific examples of how team members used the skill.

Awards can be available for team members to award their team mates to let them know what specific things they said or did to comply with the social skill for that lesson. An example would be the "Excellent Speaker Chip" given by the team to those team members complied with the social skill to speak so others in your group can hear, as in the Lesson 26: Rhyming Roundtable. For another example see Lesson 31: Sweet Similes. The Super Silent 6 award is given to partners who use a Six-Inch Voice.

Certificates can be given to each member of the class when the class reaches an established number of reward points. This helps keep families informed as to how well the students are developing their social skills. See Sample Certificates on the following pages.

Lorna Curran: *Lessons for Little Ones: Language Arts*©
Kagan Cooperative Learning • 1 (800) Wee Co-op

Kiddie Recognition Certificates

These are two of the four Kiddie Recognition Certificates available in packet of 40, on 5" x 8" assorted colored paper. See order form at back of book.

Recognition Certificates

Terrific Triad

_____

_____

_____

Perfect Partners

_____

_____

Social Skills in the Primary Classroom

This chapter provides ideas for selecting social skills, incorporating them in lessons, and keeping students focused on the social skill objectives.

Social Skills

Selection of Social Skills

When your class does a cooperative learning lesson, the decision as to which social skill to choose should be determined by the following factors. First, the students need to practice the most basic social skills of cooperative learning: Active Listening, Happy Talk and Everyone Participates. Later they need refinements, so additional social skills are introduced, one at a time, such as Paraphrasing, Strong Voices, using a Quiet, Six-Inch Voice, Quick Work, and Taking Turns.

When a social skill is first introduced, it can be quickly assimilated into group interactions. Students are reminded of the social skill frequently when it is introduced and they are given ideas as to what to do and say as they use the social skill. They become more skillful each time they use the skill if the social skill is evaluated and validated some time during each lesson. See Finger Evaluations in Chapter 4.

After initial instruction and practice of the social skills and their refinements, the social skills are determined by student needs. As the teacher observes student interactions and listens to comments made during the debriefing of a lesson, the social skill to be emphasized for the next couple of lessons usually becomes apparent. If there seemed to be an extra amount of talking and noise during a lesson and some teams didn't complete the task, if during the debriefing teams felt that some of their members were more interested in other teams' projects than in their own, then the logical choice of social skills for future lessons would be the use of Quiet, Six-Inch Voice and Everyone Participates. Possibly during the evaluation, students could issue "I Helped My Team" certificates to all team members who talked just to their teammates.

Primary Social Skills

I have found the following social skills to be the most important in primary classrooms, so they are emphasized in the lessons in this book. They are listed also in the Table of Social Skills which follows the Table of Contents.

Accepting Suggestions/Opinions Politely

❧ See Lessons 9, 13, 24, 30

When students accept each others suggestions and opinions in a polite way, everyone is much more willing to take a risk and offer an abundance of ideas some of which are unique and unusual. Offbeat and different ideas often are the ones which help the team create a superior answer or product.

Some polite ways students accept suggestions and opinions are by use of statements such as these.
"That's a neat idea."
"Great idea."
"Here is another idea."

Active Listening

❧ See Lessons 1, 3, 5, 7, 10, 16, 25, 26, 35

Active Listening is the most important of the social skills. With this skill in place, all students gain attention from the speaker. In turn, the speaker enjoys sharing the information because he knows all students are processing what has been said. Active Listening is divided into three subskills to aid the primary student. These subskills of Look, Listen, Quiet Hands are described in detail in Chapter 2.

Encouraging Statements

❧ See Lesson 29

When teams use Encouraging Statements they can gently and politely entice team members to produce more for the team. Sometimes everyone on the team has the job of making encouraging statements to all the team members. At other times one member takes the responsibility of being the Encourager. Before the lesson starts, the students can take a couple minutes to think of statements such as: "Let's all think of one more idea." or "You listened to all our ideas, now we would like an idea from you."

Everyone Participates

❧ See Lessons 12, 18, 29, 30, 34

This social skill is important to emphasize so the team knows that everyone will pull her own weight and make a contribution to the team effort. Participation by all team members can be assured in different ways. The task can be divided into parts and each team member is assigned or chooses one of the parts to do. For example, each team member draws a different story character that is used as the team does storytelling. Or everyone can work simultaneously to brainstorm rhyming words with each of the team members contributing a word to the rhyming word family that is in front of them and then passing the papers to the next person so they can add a word or each person can fit their part of the task in the proper sequence as when students place a portion of the letters into a team alphabetical order.

Happy Talk

❧ See Lessons 1, 10, 16, 25, 28, 32, 33

A very positive tone quickly develops in a classroom if students are complimenting each other while they work. This is a social skill that most students need help to develop. Happy Talk, as these compliments are called, promotes a close knit team, a wealth of ideas and brings out the best effort from all team members. Students can be given a few minutes, after they have heard an overview of the lesson, to brainstorm nice things they could say to each other. The teacher can compile quite a list from the suggestions. The Happy Talk suggestion list is added to as they complete the lesson or do additional lessons which focus on Happy Talk. The Standards Chart in Chapter 2 contains some Happy Talk statements.

Paraphrasing

✍ See Lessons 6, 22

As the students refine their speaking and listening skills, it is important that students are able to paraphrase each other so they are sure their ideas were understood. After they understand the concepts of Active Listening, second grade students may be able to move into a lesson where pairs of students take turns, one stating an opinion and their partner restating it in words that have the same meaning. For kindergarten and first grade students, I simply have them repeat what their partner said until they are capable of true paraphrasing.

Pass Papers Politely

✍ See Lesson 15

Pass Papers Politely means to be sure the person receiving the paper is ready to receive the paper. This keeps papers from accumulating in front of some team members while other team members have none. This skill is especially important during Simultaneous Roundtable (See Chapter 4). It helps reduce pressure on a particular team members because the papers are piling next to him. It also keeps the rotation in order.

Polite Suggestions

✍ See Lessons 13, 18, 19, 20, 24, 36

The teacher and a few students can model the lesson and use Polite Suggestions. The class can identify the Polite Suggestions used. These suggestions and any others the students can think of, can be recorded to make a class gambits chart. The chart is used as a reference by the students as they work together so they know what to say to each other. For K-1 students the teacher reads the list of suggestions before the lesson starts and possibly mid-way through the lesson to refresh the students' memories as to positive things they should be saying.

Strong Voices

✍ Lessons 3, 11

The social skill Strong Voices is the counter part to Active Listening. It is hard for the students to be active listeners if they have a hard time hearing the messages being sent to them. Sub skills to address while teaching students to use Strong Voices are: voice projection, sustaining the projection, enunciation, and body language. The Speak Louder hand signal described in Chapter 2 lets members of the class notify the speaker that they need improvement in the Strong Voice Skills.

Taking Turns

✍ See Lessons 14, 17

Taking turns is especially important for kindergarten and first grade students so they can learn to share supplies. It is a new experience for them to have limited supplies which necessitates Taking Turns. This social skill can be taught by having one partner have a crayon and draws the object, while the other partner has the pencil and writes the word that labels the picture. Or one partner has the scissors and cuts, while the other has the glue. They can keep the same jobs throughout the lesson or, as I prefer, have them alternate jobs so they experience different jobs.

Quick Work

* See Lessons 17, 23, 27

The Quick Work skill is important to any activities in which all teammembers' parts must fit together for the project to be complete or in a Roundtable or Roundrobin lesson where one person must complete an answer before the others can contribute their ideas. One effective way to help teams work more quickly is to have the teams analyze and share the things they did that helped them work quickly, being sure that the fastest teams shared their ideas.

Quiet, Six-Inch Voices

* See Lessons 4, 8, 21, 23, 27, 31, 35

Teams can easily do their work in an environment if the discussion of one team does not interfere with that of another team. The Quiet Voice is the skill that enables this to happen.

The Quiet Voice, or Six-Inch Voice as it is sometimes called, is easier to accomplish if several room environment features are in place:

* The team members need to be seated in such a way that they can get their work and heads close together, for

example; being seated across a narrow table, around a single student desk, or around a piece of tagboard on the floor.

* The teams should have a 3 to 4 foot space between them so it is possible to keep their own team's ideas to themselves. When a team first starts using Quiet Voices, the team can have a prompter who listens and reminds any members who need a softer voice.

How Social Skills Work In A Lesson

To help students understand how a social skill works within a lesson, the students, after hearing an overview of the lesson, are given an opportunity to brainstorm some things that would be said or done to achieve the social skill in that particular lesson. Their ideas are recorded and used as a basis for evaluating their success in having accomplished that social skill. For example, before using the social skill of Active Listening, the teacher lists student suggestions as to what the students should do and say to be good active listeners. Some examples of ideas they offer are provided in the box on next page.

Social Skills Phrases Chart

If accomplishing the social skill would be enhanced by using specific phrases or behaviors, the class makes a chart of those "gambits" before they start the lesson. If the social skill is to encourage others, the class would make a list of phrases that would remind their team members to do their best, such as:

* "You look like you have an idea, what is it?"

- "Everyone started right away."
- "That's terrific that you are making your pictures so neat."

Review of the Social Skills Chart

If the lesson uses a social skill that has been used in a previous lesson, the chart of phrases from the previous lesson should be reviewed after the students have heard an overview of the new lesson to see which phrases on the chart are applicable to this lesson.

Additions to the Social Skills Chart

At the end of each lesson, time can be provided for students to add new phrases that they used in the course of the lesson. Soon the students have a variety of phrases to use for each of the social skills they would use as they work in their teams.

Continued Focus on Social Skills

Another factor that leads to successful use of the social skill is to keep the students aware of the social skill as they work through the lesson. As the lesson starts and the students hear the directions for doing the lesson, they receive a quick reminder of the social skill. "Remember, as you discuss with your partners today, you will be paraphrasing each other so you will know you understand what each other is saying." After the students have been involved in the lesson for a couple of minutes, they can be reminded of the social skill in several ways.

Teacher Quotes

The teacher can interrupt the lesson and quote phrases heard, then praise and reward the teams or class for using the phrases.

Reflection Time

During the lesson, the teacher can give the teams an opportunity to reflect and see if they have used any of the gambits from the chart. They could volunteer to share those they used.

Refer to Gambits Chart

The teacher rereads the gambit chart so the teams can decide which of the phrases from the chart they would like to try to use.

Active Listening
Student Responses

Do
Look at the speaker.
Nod your head.
Smile.
Lean toward the speaker.

Say
"That's great."
"I like that."
"Good idea."
"Yes, I like that too."

Reminders

The teacher reminds the students that they will be evaluating their use of the social skill at the end of the lesson so they should be sure to use at least two of the phrases while they work together.

Record and Praise Phrases

The teacher should make a point of recording phrases used and purposely stand near teams that need encouragement to use the social skill.

Evaluation & Debriefing of Social Skills

At the end of the lesson, the social skill should be evaluated. The students need a way to signal or record their score. See Debriefing in Chapter 3 and Evaluation Structures in Chapter 4.

Cooperative Learning Structures

Color-Coded Co-op Cards[1]

❧ See Lessons 16, 23, 25, 26.

This structure is best done in the primary grades first with partners and then with groups of four. When doing Color Coded Coop Cards with partners, each partner is given a set of 5 or 6 colored cards, a different color for each partner. The cards can either be pre-printed or the students can print the information on the cards. Types of information that can be printed on the cards to help reinforce language arts are: a) alphabet letters; b) vocabulary words for recognition; c) vocabulary words and definitions for recognition and meaning; d) abbreviations and the words they stand for. After the cards are made, partner #1 hands his cards to partner #2. Partner #2 shows the cards one by one to partner #1. All the cards that are said correctly are marked with a happy face and placed in a pile on the floor. When a card is answered incorrectly, person #2 teaches the letter or word to person #1 and

returns the card to his hand to show again. If neither of the partners can remember the information on the card, they are to both raise their hands and the teacher can give them the information they need. After person #1 has learned all his cards, the partners reverse roles so partner #1 shows the cards and teaches the information to Person #2. Doing Color-Coded Co-op Cards with teams of 4 is very similar. While persons #1 and #2 are paired up studying, persons #3 and #4 are following the same procedure. When both sets of partners finish their studying, the teams can form new study partners with persons #1 and #4 working together and persons #2 and #3 working together to review the material to check that they remember all the information.

Community Circle

❧ See Lessons 1, 3, 4

During Community Circle, students sit in a large circle so that each student is able to see all the other students. One

---

1. For further information on these and other structures, see Spencer Kagan's book *Cooperative Learning.* Note: some of the descriptions of the structures here have been simplified considerably from the original forms created by Kagan. For example, Color-Coded Co-op Cards, as developed by Kagan, has ten steps and includes built-in improvement scoring; Partners in the original form also has ten steps.

person, usually the teacher, is the leader and starts the Community Circle by stating an open ended sentence that everyone will answer by completing the sentence with an answer that expresses their own likes, dislikes, feelings, or knowledge of the topic. For example, the teacher might use the sentence, "My favorite food is...." Everyone is given a minute to think of the ending they will use for the sentence. The social skill is stated such as active listening or speaking so others can hear you. The leader completes the sentence and the turn passes to the right until all students have had their turn. If they can't think of an answer when it is their turn, they say "Pass." This means after all the other students have had their turn, they will be expected to have their answer ready to share. After everyone has shared, the students evaluate how well they used the social skill.

Double Community Circle

As soon as the students are comfortable doing Community Circle as a total class, the class can then be divided into two equal groups, which will each do the Community Circle simultaneously. The teacher still states the topic and demonstrates the format of the response sentence. Then a student starter is designated for each circle. Those students give their responses and the turns continue to the right around each of the circles. The teacher selects a position midway between the two circles to observe and facilitate as necessary. Each circle does its own evaluation of the social skill but the validation of the score and the debriefing of the lesson can be done with both groups by alternately calling on students from each circle to answer questions. A plus for Double Community Circle is that it takes less time. A disadvantage is that students don't have an opportunity to hear all responses.

Cooperative Projects

✒ See Lessons 9, 28, 30, 32, 33, 34

Cooperative Projects are used most frequently in the primary grades with groups of two, three or four students. After students have worked in pairs and are used to sharing the responsibility of developing a product, it is easy for them to do similar activities with more students in the group.

A. Partner Projects

Partners work together to complete a project. Their projects have tasks that are in multiples of two so they can each do half of the jobs. They can either decide how they will share the tasks or the tasks can be assigned.

Partners works well with primary students whose attention span is short. When they need to take turns giving ideas or sharing equipment, their turn come quickly and often, helping to keep them focused on the lesson. Also, it helps their attention during discussions

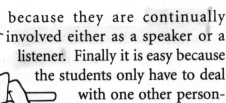

because they are continually involved either as a speaker or a listener. Finally it is easy because the students only have to deal with one other personality besides their own. A caution though, is that partners need to be put together carefully so that two abrasive personalities are not put together. Also, if there are students in class with poorly developed interpersonal skills, partners need to be changed frequently so that class will share the responsibility of working with these students. They will share the responsibility of being role models and showing them how members should work together.

B. Team Projects

Students are put together to work in groups or teams of three to six students. The number of students may depend on the number of tasks necessary to complete the project. Usually the largest number recommended for primary students is four. More students than this makes for too many interactions which is difficult for young children. With more than four students on a team, shy children are reluctant to participate. Often the team will split into two separate groups who tend to disagree, instead of functioning as a single cooperative unit. Sometimes I do use teams of six if the students are putting together a project that has six distinctive parts such as in Lesson 28: Rosie's Walk, where the teams recreate this story that has six parts. Some projects are short such as finding the answer to a story problem or lining

up by birth date. Other projects may be more involved such as surveying class interests and making a graph to record the information. If the team does need to make a product, it helps assure success for each team if they have the talents with in the team that are necessary to complete the product.

The procedure for doing cooperative projects is:

- Students are arranged in teams whose size is determined by the number of tasks or parts to the lesson.
- The teacher presents the directions for completing the project, orally and with a chart or overhead.
- Each team member completes his/her part of the project, receiving advice and assistance from the rest of the team.
- Cooperative projects are assembled and shared with other students.

Corners

- See Lessons 2, 4, 5, 29

The students find out about themselves and others by selecting which of four choices would be their favorite choice. They can choose which of four types of animals they would prefer to be if they were an animal. They could choose which of the four times of day they like most. A sign labeling each choice is hung in each corner of the room. The students write down their choice. They go to the corner for that choice. They can share reasons for selecting that choice.

Eight Square

Eight square is an information gathering structure. The students are given a paper that has been divided into eight sections. They are given directions as to the type of information they are to gather. Each person then moves about the room to find a student who will sign his/her name in a square and provide some of the information needed. Each square must be filled in by a different student so they continue moving around the room, asking students to add information to the sheet, until all the squares are filled or until time is called. Some types of information that can be gathered are; colors of clothes, letters of the alphabet, numbers, addition facts or spelling words. A perfect social skill to practice while using this structure is the use of please and thank you. The students evaluate whether everyone who asked them to fill in a square used please as they asked and used thank you after the information had been given. The information can be shared by calling on any student to tell the name and information from one of the squares on his/ her paper. The person whose name was in that square is the next person to read the information from a square on his/her paper. The students are to call the names of only those students who have not yet been called on to share. If a person has no new names to call when it is his/her turn, then those students who have not yet had a turn, raise their hands and one of those students is chosen to continue the sharing.

Evaluation Structures

✍ See all lessons

Sometime during the lesson, the social skill should be evaluated. The students need a way to signal or record their score.

Finger Evaluations

The scores can be signaled by giving a certain number of fingers a particular value. Five fingers can mean everyone did the social skill, three fingers can mean most people did the social skill, and one finger can mean we were so busy with the activity that we forgot to do the social skill.

Evaluation Slips

Scores can be written down on small pieces of paper and shared with the team or the class.

Group Evaluations

The skill can be evaluated by individual students, by teams who agree on a score, or by taking an average of the individual scores on their team.

Teacher Evaluations

The teacher can arrive at a score or validate students' scores by giving specific examples of what was observed while the teams worked.

Think Time

Students should also be given time to think of reasons for their scores. Then

Lorna Curran: *Lessons for Little Ones: Language Arts*©
Kagan Cooperative Learning • 1 (800) Wee Co-op

students can be called on to validate their score to the class, or students can share reasons within their teams, or students can pair up to share their reasons.

Formations

❧ See Lesson 18

The students use their bodies to form simple shapes such as geometric shapes, numbers, or letters. The teacher draws the shapes the teams should make or tells them the shape they are to make. Then, the teams or class discuss how to make the formation, which students will become which part of that formation, and then they take their places to make the assigned formation. The teacher or teammates may assign one teammember to be a Checker to see if their team has created the right shape, or if it needs some modifications.

Group Discussion

❧ See Lessons 5, 9, 12, 15, 25

Group Discussion is used when each team needs to have time to gather information or to come to consensus on an idea. The team members are seated close together so it is easy for them to share ideas with each other. If the conversation is dominated by a few of the team members or if some of the team members are reluctant to contribute, the structure Talking Chips may be used along with Group Discussion to assure equal opportunity for contributing ideas.

Inside-Outside Circle

a. Individual Inside-Outside Circle

❧ See Lessons 6, 31

Inside Outside Circle is an excellent structure for simultaneous sharing of information. Half the students form an inner circle and half the students form an outer circle. Students stand or sit facing a partner. The students first share with their partner. Then the students in the inner circle stay in place while the students in the outer circle move an indicated number of spaces to their right to find a new partner. For kindergarten students I have 12" x18" carpet scraps that the outer circle students sit on that clearly mark the spaces. They count the carpet scraps as they move. They continue sharing and moving on signal until an appropriate amount of material has been shared.

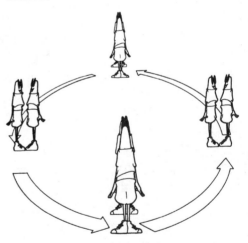

b. Team Inside-Outside Circle

❧ See Lessons 12, 28, 29, 30, 31, 32

Each team stands together in an Inside-

Outside Circle, that is, four teams in a circle facing in, and four teams in another circle facing out, with each team facing another team. Teams do a presentation to each other, they then take planning time to evaluate and improve their presentation. Next the inside circle rotates clockwise to the next team. Teams present again. With successive rotations, teams improve their presentations considerably. The inner circle teams keep sharing and moving until they return to their original position. So the primary students will have an easy time knowing which direction to move, it helps to tape cards with direction arrows to the floor.

Jigsaw

❧ See Lessons 10, 12

Jigsaw can be a very difficult structure for primary students to use if it is done too soon before the students have had some opportunities to develop strategies for working together. It is an easy structure to use in primary grades, if the students have had several opportunities to successfully participate in team building, communication building, and mastery structures. The team building structures will have developed accountability and a sense of trust, which is necessary if team members are depending upon each other to learn information that the team needs to complete their project. The communication building structures give them the skills they need in order to be able to share the information they learned with their team. The mastery structures give

the teams the strategies they need to be effective students and teachers as each team member teaches the rest of the team the information which was learned in his expert group.

If Jigsaw is done before the students are comfortable doing the types of structures mentioned above, the lesson could easily fail because the students don't possess the interpersonal skills necessary to work with two different groups, gather information, learn that information, and teach that information all within one lesson. If the structure is used in the primary classroom later in the year when the students have the necessary skills, it is a fun way for them to learn a lot of different information in a short amount of time.

The procedure for doing Jigsaw is as follows. Each team member is assigned to an expert group. For primary students I like each team to have an envelope of pictures. Each picture in the envelope represents one of the expert groups. Each team member takes out a picture and takes it to the expert group. Each expert group learns the part of the information assigned to them. The expert group members then each take this information back to their teams. Each team member teaches the team the information learned in the expert group. Kindergarten and first grade students can take the information in oral or pictorial form. The team then uses the information gained from each of their team members to complete the team activity.

Line-Ups

A. Characteristics Line-Ups

✍ See Lesson 19

In a Characteristic Line-Up, the teacher lays a tape or yarn on the floor and labels sections with answer choices. The students decide which choice is the best one for them and arrange themselves in the proper order on the line. The teacher reads the labels at each end of the line and any labels that are placed along the length of the line. The line could be labeled so the students would line up by the month of their birthday, by the number that shows how many members there are in their family, or to show what time they got up in the morning. The students write down their answers on a small piece of paper. They take the paper with them to the line up and stand in the section that has the same label as the word on their small paper. They can use the results of the line up to make a graph. Also, the students in each section can discuss advantages and disadvantages of their answer. For example, they discuss the advantages and disadvantages of having a large or small family.

b. Value Line-Up

✍ See Lessons 6, 7, 8

One end of the line represents like, the other end represents dislike. Once the line is labeled, students line up according to how much they like or dislike something, or as to whether they agree or disagree with something.

Students stand closer to the ends or closer to the middle according to how much they liked or disliked the idea or object being discussed. Other ideas for Line-Ups are: happy/sad; agree/disagree; a lot/some/none; yes/maybe/no. Students in a Value Line-Up can discuss reasons for their opinion. They can number from 1 to 4 along the line-up to talk to other students with similar opinions. The #1 student talks with the #2 student next to him, while the #3 student talks with the #4 student next to him. In order to have students talk to others with different opinions, they can do the Split and Slide or The Wrap.

c. The Split and Slide

✍ See Lesson 9

To discover reasons given for a different view point, students can do the Split and Slide. For the Split and Slide, count the students to establish equal halves of the line. Have one half of the line stay standing on the line. Have the other half of the line up take two steps forward to create two separate lines. Have the students in each of the lines number themselves in order along the line, having the numbering go in the same direction in each of the lines. Then have the new line move in front of the established line until the students are standing face to face with the person who has the same number. Kindergarten and first graders actually need to hold the number card or need to be carefully directed to their partner. Now the students are facing someone who has a different view point than they do and they are ready for a discussion.

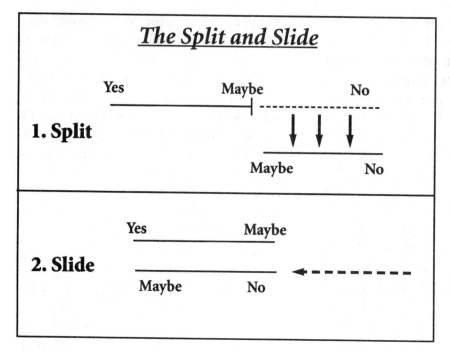

The Split and Slide

1. Split

Yes   Maybe   No

Maybe   No

2. Slide

Yes   Maybe

Maybe   No

d. The Wrap

🍂 See Lesson 9

To have some of the students talk to people who have an opinion opposite their own, have the students do The Wrap. To do The Wrap, (sometimes called a Folded Value Line), one end of the line comes down to meet the other end of the line. This makes partners of the first person at each end of the line; the second people from each end also become partners, and so on along the line. The end partners talk about extreme opposite opinions, but the students who were in the middle of the line up are discussing with someone who has very similar opinions.

The Wrap

Yes   Maybe

No   Maybe

e. The Split Class Line-Up

🍂 See Lesson 9

Sometimes I have half the class make one Line-Up, and the other half of the class stands in another Line-Up. This is particularly useful in primary grades, because there are not so many students in each line and it makes it easier for the students to find their place. Also when it is time to discuss with a partner, the two lines just move toward each other and automatically the students have their partners.

f. Team Line-Ups

🍂 See Lesson 20

Team Line-Ups are done just like Class Line-Ups except only teammates are in the Line-Up. Sometimes the team members stand on the line to show the order or value of just a few ideas. Other times, like in the lesson like in Lesson 12, they can show many ideas by leaving markers that represent their ideas.

Numbered Heads Together

🍂 See Lessons 13, 21, 25, 26, 27, 36

Numbered Heads Together is a structure which encourages a team to consider many ideas and then

share the most appropriate answer. Numbered Heads together has the following components. The students in each team are numbered. The teacher asks a question, the teammates put their heads together to discuss possible answers, and the team agrees which is the correct or best answer, making sure each team member knows that answer. The teacher says a number. The person on each team that has that number raises their hand, ready to answer the question. In Sequential Numbered Heads together, only one person at a time is called upon. In Simultaneous Numbered Heads Together, all the students with the number have the opportunity to respond at once.

Forms of Simultaneous Numbered Heads Together

When primary students first start using Numbered Heads Together, I use information that could be answered with a limited number of predetermined alternatives and can easily be signaled by showing the correct number of fingers, or I provide the team with a set of answer cards. The team decides what would be the best solution or answer and then signals the answer by holding up a card or by showing the number of fingers that represents the best answer.

This makes coming to agreement easier, because, first of all, it limits the number of answer choices. Also, no one feels attachment to a particular answer because it was an answer provided by the teacher rather than by one of them. Some students become very attached to an answer because it was their idea and have a hard time accepting the fact that it was not the answer chosen by the team. Finally sharing the answers becomes very quick and easy because all teams can show the answer at the same time.(See Lesson 21: Who Did It)

Partners

✍ See Lessons 2, 3, 14, 25, 31

The procedure for doing Partners is simple. The teacher pairs up the students. They are given a task that they must work on together to complete. The partners can decide how they will share the task, or the tasks can be assigned. After completing the task and deciding how to share, the partners group with other partners and all participate in sharing their products. Pairs seem to be the best grouping to start with in primary grades. It is easy for the young students whose attention span is short because when it is a task where students need to take turns giving ideas or using equipment, their turn comes quickly and often, helping to keep them focused on the lesson. Also it helps their attention during discussions because they are both continually involved either as a speaker or a listener. Finally, it is easy because the students only have to deal with one other personality besides their own. A caution to consider though is that pairs need to be put together carefully so that two abrasive personalities are not put together to do a partner project. Also if there are students in the class with poorly developed interpersonal skills, pairs need to be changed frequently so several people will have the job of working with and being these students role models, showing how students should work together.

Rotating Reporters

❦ See Lessons 24, 28, 32, 33, 35

For Rotating Reporters, one or more team members move to another team to share the team product or answer. The procedure is as follows: Team members all practice how to share the team information, team members are numbered, the teacher chooses one or more numbers and members with those numbers become the Roving Reporters who rotate to one or more teams to share the team information. With several rotations, team members become more practiced in sharing.

Roundtable

a. Sequential Roundtable

❦ See Lessons 9, 17, 27, 33, 35

During Sequential Roundtable, the students all contribute ideas to one sheet of paper. The team members need to know the order or direction in which the paper and pencil will be passed. Primary students usually need a minute or so to practice the passing order before they begin the Roundtable. When the signal to begin is given, a team member quickly writes or draws an idea and then passes the paper and pencil to the next person so they can add an answer. The students continue adding answers and passing the paper until the time to stop is announced. Usually in primary grades, there are no more than 4 students per team. The teammates need to sit close together so it is easy for them to pass the paper. Also, teammates are sometimes allowed to suggest answers to each other if they need help. Because they are seated close together, teams can converse without disturbing the teams around them.

b. Signaled Sequential Roundtable

Signaled Sequential Roundtable is done exactly like Sequential Roundtable except for one change. Before a group member draws or writes an answer, the answer is told to the team members. If they agree that it would be an acceptable answer for the topic, they will give the thumbs up signal. If any team member thinks the answer is not correct, he/she will give a thumb sideways signal which means talk it over. If, after talking it over, the team decides the original answer is right, that answer is recorded. Many times after the person who suggested the answer explains their reason for choosing that answer, the team agrees that the answer is correct. If the team feels another answer is needed, then the person contributes an another answer or asks for suggestions for an alternative answer from the team. When agreement is reached and all team members have thumbs up, then the answer is recorded. An advantage of Signaled Sequential Roundtable is that all the team members know immediately what all the answers on the recording sheet mean. Also, because each person needs to give the signal before an answer can be recorded, it keeps all team members focused on the lesson even if it is not their turn to draw or write.

C. Simultaneous Roundtable

This structure is the same as Sequential Roundtable except, each student has a paper. Each team member writes an answer at the same time and then passes the paper to the next person on the team. Primary students need to focus both on working quickly themselves, but also on waiting politely until the next person is ready. Sometimes only two or three papers are passed in a group of four.

Roundrobin

✍ See Lessons 11, 12, 29, 34

Roundrobin is like Roundtable — each student in turn contributes an answer for the group. The difference is that with Roundrobin the answers are oral rather than written.

Stand and Share

✍ See Lessons 24, 25

Stand and Share is used to involve everyone in the sharing of team answers. In preparation for Stand and Share, the teams should have discussed until they agree upon an answer or set of answers for their team. Then I use several different versions of Stand and Share to have my students share their answers.

a. Numbered Stand and Share

This type of sharing is valuable when each team may have several different answers that can be shared. The team-members number off so each has a different number. The teacher calls out a number and the person from each team with this number stands up. These students standing are responsible for sharing one of their team's answers when their team is called on, and they are seated as soon as they have shared an answer. Call out another number and a different person from each team stands to share another answer the team had agreed upon. Continue this process until all the teams have shared all their answers. A variation of the Numbered Stand and Share is to call on only one or two teams each time a number is called. This way not every person shares when their number is called but they must be ready to answer which keeps them focused on the answers. This variation is good when there are not quite so many possible answers that could be shared.

b. Whole Class Stand and Share

The second type of Stand and Share has the whole class stand up when it is time to share. A person from each team is called on to share an answer. When that answer is shared, that team and any other team that had the same answer, sit down. Continue sharing answers until all teams sit down. This type of Stand and Share is best used when each team agrees on just one or two possible answers to be shared.

Talking Chips

❧ See Lesson 29

Talking Chips are tokens or paper markers distributed equally to all team members, usually three or four per member. Every time a team member contributes a comment or idea, he must put one of his

talking chips into a team pile. When he has spent all his chips he cannot offer any more ideas until all the other team members have spent all their chips. Then the chips can be redistributed so more ideas can be gathered. If students are limited to one chip each and there is a rule that students place their chips in the center as they speak and can only gather them back when all chips are used, the structure forces all students to participate each round.

Team Interviews

❧ See Lesson 9

One teammate is selected to be interviewed by the rest of the team. Team Interviews are good ways to have one team member share his/her thoughts, accomplishments, and plans for a project. Team Interviews in which a team member role plays a character from the story, allow the students to gain detailed information about that character.

Teams Share

❧ See Lessons 5, 13, 17, 31, 33

For Teams Share, each team in the class is paired up with another team. These sets of teams meet together to share the answers or products that are the result of them having completed their team activity. For the first few times primary students do Team Share together, I pass out sets of Team Share identification cards so each team gets a visual message as to which teams meet together. One team would get a red card marked #1, another team gets a red card marked #2. These two teams meet together with the first team sharing first while the second team is the audience. Then the second team shares and the first team is the audience. The same procedure would be happening with the two blue teams, green teams, etc. If there are uneven numbers of teams, I either group three teams together to share or I become the audience for one of the teams.

Think-Pair-Share

❧ See Lessons 2, 3, 14, 18, 19, 22, 31

Think-Pair-Share is one of the most frequently used cooperative learning structures for two reasons. One, it is so easy to

use. Two, it immediately involves everyone in a class discussion. The procedure for Think-Pair-Share is as follows: Remind the students who their established partner is or have them quickly find a partner by making eye contact or touching someone next to them. Then the teacher asks a question. The students are given a minute or two to think of their own answer. The students pair up and discuss their answers with their partners. The teacher gives the silent signal.

The students are then given an opportunity to share with the class any ideas they said or heard. Directions to the students might sound like this:

- "Think about this question inside your head."
- "Turn to your partner and pair up to tell each other your ideas."
- "Would anyone like to share an idea they said or heard?"

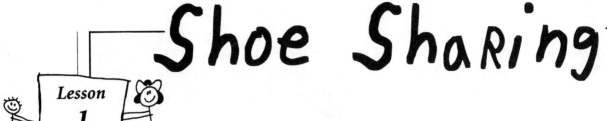

Shoe Sharing

• Literature

Shoes

• Grade Level

K-2

• Type of Lesson

Sharing Ideas: Travel Plans

• Cognitive Objective

Each person shares an idea about where they would like to go in their shoes.

• Social Skills Objective

Active Listening

• Materials

Active Listening Chart, and if you don't have carpeting in your classroom, you might like to have a large blanket the students can sit around, or collect carpet samples for the students to sit on.

- **Community Circle**
- **Class Discussion**

Structures

Background Information

The students have heard or read the story *Shoes* by Elizabeth Winthrop. The students will have seen the Active Listening Chart (included) and have discussed the three parts of Active Listening.

Lesson Overview:

"Students, today we will be sitting in a circle, talking about our shoes. Each of us will have a turn to speak; all the rest of us need to use Active Listening."

Lesson Sequence

Teacher Instruction:

Teach Active Listening

"Before we do the Community Circle, let us find out what Active Listening is.

Look at the Active Listening Chart (see Chapter 2 page 12). The eyes on the chart tell us that we need to look at the person who is speaking. The picture of the ears tell us that we need to listen to the words that are said and think about what they mean. The hands show us that we need to have our hands folded together in our lap so they won't bother us or anyone else."

Community Circle:

Ideas About Where to Go in Shoes

A. Preparation of Circle

"Come quietly and make a large circle. Make sure that you can see all the other students. Check the Active Listening Chart to see if your eyes are looking at the speaker, your ears are listening to the words, and your hands are folded together in your lap so they don't bother anybody. Remember to use Active Listening all the time we are in the Community Circle because at the end we will think about how well we used Active Listening."

B. State Community Circle Topic
"Today we will think about where we would like to go in our shoes. If you could go any place you wanted to go in your shoes, where would you go?"

Curran's Comments:

Community Circle is the first cooperative learning structure I use. The main objective of the lesson is to give the students practice being active listeners. When Active Listening is in place, the students feel comfortable speaking because they know they will have an attentive audience. To be an effective active listener you have to be able to hear the speaker, so this necessitates the initiation of a second goal, to be a clear speaker. At the beginning of the year, I use Community Circle often until I am sure all the students know how to be good listeners and speakers. It can be used with a variety of topics, some of which are discussed at the end of this lesson.

C. Model Response Form
The teacher models the correct form for responding to the question by answering first. The person to the teacher's right will answer next. Continue around the circle until everyone has answered, or used the right to pass.

D. Right to Pass
If any students cannot think of an answer when it is their turn, they may say, "Pass." After all the students have had their turns, go back around the circle and give the students that passed, a time to give their answer. After having this extra thinking time, they are expected to answer.

Finger Evaluation:
Use of Active Listening
"Think about how we used Active Listening today. In a few minutes you will signal how well you think we did. If you think all of us used Active Listening, you will show five fingers. If you think most of us used Active Listening, you will show three fingers. If you think just a few of us used Active Listening, you will show one finger. When I say 'one, two, three, show,' have your hand right in front of your chest and put up the correct number of fingers to show your answer. 'One, two, three, show." Ask several students to validate their signal by telling about things they saw and heard that let them know if the class used Active Listening.

Finger Evaluation:
Use of Sharing
Ask the students to show thumbs up/down if they think everyone shared about their shoes.

Curran's Comments:

When the students validate the cognitive or social skill objectives by giving examples of things they saw or heard, they are reminded to use the words, "someone" or "somebody" instead of using specific names. This keeps them from putting pressure on any individual.

Class Discussion:

Debrief the Lesson

To find out how the students felt about the lesson have them discuss some of the following questions:

- How did you feel while you were waiting for your turn to share?
- How did you feel after your turn was over?
- How did you feel if someone said the same thing you were planning to say?
- Do you think it is all right for someone to change to a different answer if their answer has already been said? Why?
- Is it all right to keep your answer the same if someone says it before you have a chance to give the answer? Why?
- How did it feel to have everyone listening to you?
- How did it feel to use Active Listening while the other students were speaking?

Variations:

- You might like to do each of the three parts of Active Listening as separate social skills, doing just eye contact for the first day, doing listening to the words another day, and finally doing hands in your lap.
- After the social skills have been learned, dividing the class into two or three Community Circles which all share at the same time, makes the sharing time go faster. Students should have an adult or an upper grade tutor as a facilitator as they are learning the Active Listening standards. See Double Community Circle, Chapter 4.

Other Applications:

- Students discuss a favorite thing that happened at school today.
- Have them share their favorite part of a story or movie.
- Have them share what they like to do on the weekend or after school.
- As a pretest, have each student share one thing they know about a topic such as the zoo. Ideas that are not mentioned in the circle, you know you have to teach.
- As a post test, have each student share one thing they learned about the topic. If some facts taught are not mentioned, they can be considered for reteaching.
- Have them think about what they would like to know about a topic before the class starts exploring that topic.
- Pick another article of clothing: coats, hats, socks, etc.

Extensions:

- Do Lesson 2: A Place for Partners, which has pairs of students agree on a place where they would like to go in their shoes. Then they draw a picture of themselves at that place.

Community Circle Topics

I like the T.V. program _____Because_____

My favorite food is _____

After school I like to _____

When I grow up I would like to _____

If I could have a wish I would wish for _____

The funniest thing I can think of is _____

My favorite story is _____ because _____

The zoo animal I would like to take care of is the _____

because _____

This is what I remember about bears. They _____

The things I liked best today was _____

I feel unhappy when _____

One thing I would like to fix is _____

During vacation I _____

I would like to find out _____ about _____

Lorna Curran: *Lessons for Little Ones: Language Arts*©
Kagan Cooperative Learning • 1 (800) Wee Co-op

A Place for Partners

• Literature
Shoes

• Grade Level
K-2

• Type of Lesson
Sharing Ideas: Create a product to share

• Cognitive Objective
Partners draw a picture of a place they both agree they would like to go to in their shoes.

• Social Skills Objective
Happy Talk

• Materials
Drawing Paper and Crayons

Structures
- Class Discussion
- Community Circle
- Partners
- Think-Pair-Share

Background Information

The students have heard the story *Shoes* by Elizabeth Winthrop. They have discussed places where they would like to go (Lesson 1: Shoe Sharing, could be used to collect ideas) or they could do a Roundrobin brainstorm to think of places they would like to go.

Lesson Overview

"You will work with a partner to choose a place both of you would like to go. Then both of you will work together to draw a picture of this place. Finally you will share your picture with the class. While you work together, you will use Happy Talk."

Lesson Sequence

Class Discussion:

Ideas for Happy Talk

Either read phrases for a Happy Talk Chart that was made from a previous lesson or create a happy talk chart as the students tell you nice things they would say to each other as they work together. Some suggestions they might offer are: "Good idea!" "Nice drawing." "That's neat."

Partners:

Picture of Where To Go

A. Preparation for Partners

Arrange the class into partners. Each pair is given a piece of drawing paper and crayons.

B. Partner Discussion: Place to Go

"Partners, you need to talk about places you would like to go and agree on a place you both would like to go. The ideas you heard during Community Circle will help you think of some places you could go."

C. Partner Project: Make Partner Picture

"Remember, you need to show just one place and both of you need to be in the picture with your shoes. Share the job of drawing the picture and give each other Happy Talk statements as you work together."

Pause and Praise:
Check for Happy Talk

Walk around the room recording Happy Talk statements. After students have worked for about five minutes, ask students if they have used any Happy Talk statements yet. If they have, ask for three or four volunteers to share what they have said. Share with them any Happy Talk statements you heard. "You have ten more minutes to finish your picture and decide which of you will hold the picture and which one will tell about the picture during sharing time. Continue to use Happy Talk as you finish the picture and remember the nice things that were said."

Think-Pair-Share:
Evaluate Happy Talk

Have the students show Active Listening. "Think about some of the Happy Talk your partner said while you worked together. Tell your partner what Happy Talk you heard them use." Give students two or three minutes to share this information. "Show thumbs up if you could tell your partner some Happy Talk they used." Praise or reward according to how many thumbs you saw. Have the students share any new Happy Talk statements that were used and add them to the Happy Talk Chart.

Community Circle:
Share the Pictures

The students sit next to their partners as they make a large circle. Have a Community Circle Sharing by using the lesson plan for Sharing Shoes. Instead of telling about their shoes, they will tell about their picture. "Remember that one of you will be telling about the picture, while the other person is holding the pic-

---

Curran's Comments:

Sometimes you will not hear any Happy Talk for several minutes. When that happens, I stop the students when I hear the first Happy Talk statement and tell them,"I just heard a Happy Talk statement. Jason said, 'That's a great idea.' I'm going to put a reward point on our class chart because Jason and his partner were the first ones to get us started with Happy Talk today." That usually starts a flood of Happy Talk. Then you are very busy recording all the positive statements you hear.

Every so often, I don't hear any Happy Talk. Then I either stop them and reread the Happy Talk Chart, or pretend I hear a Happy Talk statement. In that case I would say, "It is so nice when I hear people saying things like 'Wonderful idea.' and 'Terrific coloring.' I am going to continue to listen for nice things that are said." Again this will start Happy Talk from most of the class.

---

ture. The rest of the class is to do Active Listening."

Think-Pair-Share:
Debrief the Lesson
Find out how the students felt about the lesson by discussing some of the following questions.

- How did you and your partner find a place where both of you wanted to go?
- How did you share the job of drawing the picture?
- How did it feel when you said nice things to each other?
- How did you decide who would talk and who would share the picture?

Variations:

- When the students share the picture, you can let them decide how the picture will be shared as long as both of them help with the job.

- If you want everyone to speak, the directions can say that both people need to hold the picture and tell about it.
- Older students may be required to write a sentence or two that tells about their picture.

Extensions:

- The partners can make up a story of what happened to them when they went to the place in their picture.
- Students can think of a storybook character to be their pretend partner and tell where they would like to go with that storybook character.
- The partners can make a booklet, chart, or collage of fun places to go.
- The partners can make a list of places they both have been.
- Make a class graph that shows the type of places the students chose to go with their partner.

Sharing Sensational Sections of Stories

• Literature
Any Story where you would like students to be able to retell their favorite part.

• Grade Level
K-2

• Type of Lesson
Sharing Ideas: Favorite Part of a Story.

• Cognitive Objective
Make a picture and tell about your favorite part of a story.

• Social Skills Objective
Strong Voices; Active Listening

• Materials
Drawing paper, crayons, and color cards (3" x4") to designate different Community Circles.

Structures
- *Class Discussion*
- *Double Community Circle*
- *Think-Pair-Share*

Background Information
The students have heard a story at least twice; once to enjoy the story and a second time to listen for their favorite part of the story.

Lesson Overview
"We have just heard a story and have listened for our favorite part. Now we are going to draw a picture of that part and be ready to tell the class what is happening. As you tell about the part of the story you like, you will need to use a voice that the rest of us can easily hear."

Lesson Sequence
Class Discussion:
Using a Voice that is Easy to Hear
"What are some things we can do that will make it easy for others to hear us?"

The students may provide answers similar to these: "Look at the people you are talking to." "Use a loud voice." "Talk so we can understand the words." Write down their answers so they can refer to them as they evaluate the lesson and so they can use the list when they do other lessons in which you want to emphasize being a good speaker.

Independent Activity:
Make the Picture
Give the students ten to fifteen minutes to draw their pictures. While they draw,

Curran's Comments:
If I have parent helpers, I have them help me write the sentences. Sometimes I borrow fifth or sixth grade students who like to help during their recess, or when they have finished their class work.

---

you can ask them to tell you a sentence about their picture so you can write it at the top or bottom of the picture.

Double Community Circle:

Share Pictures

When most of the students have finished their pictures, pass out two different colors of color cards to designate which Community Circle the students will go to. "Students who have the red cards will make a large circle over here by the red piece of construction paper. The students who have the blue cards will make a large circle by the blue piece of construction paper. Bring your pictures with you to the circle." Make each circle large enough so the few students who are finishing their pictures will be able to find a place to sit. "Show Active Listening by putting your picture down on the floor in front of you. Remember to do all parts of Active Listening by looking at the speaker, really listening to what is being said, and by keeping your hands in your lap so they won't bother you or anyone else. When it is your turn to share, you will pick up your picture to hold in front of your chest while you tell us about your favorite part of the story. Use a loud, clear speaking voice as you share. The rest of us will remember to use active listening." Choose a student in each circle to start the sharing. The person to their right will share next. Continue around the circles until all have shared. Check around the circles to see if there are any late comers who need to have a turn.

Finger Signal Evaluation:

Use of Speaking

"Let's see how well we did in speaking so others can hear. In a minute you will signal how well you think the speakers did. If you think all the speakers were easy to hear, you will show five fingers. If you think most of the speakers were easy to hear, you will show three fingers. If you think just a few of the speakers were easy to hear, you will show one finger. Be ready to tell a reason for the number of fingers you are showing. When I say 'One, two, three show,' have your hand right in front of your chest and put up the right number of fingers to show your answer." Ask several students to validate their answer by telling things they saw and heard that let them know that the people were or were not easy to hear.

Class Evaluation:

Sharing of Pictures

Double check to see that everyone showed the picture and told about their favorite part of the story. If everyone participated, they can applaud their efforts.

Think-Pair-Share:

Debrief the Lesson

Find out how the students felt about doing the lesson by discussing some of the following questions.

* How did it feel to share your picture with the class?
* What did we do today that made it easy to speak so others could easily hear you?

Lorna Curran: *Lessons for Little Ones: Language Arts*©

Kagan Cooperative Learning • 1 (800) Wee Co-op

- What would make it easier for you to speak clearly next time?
- How did you feel while you were waiting for your turn?
- How did you feel when your turn was over?
- What would make it easier to listen to the others tell about their favorite part of the story?

Extensions:

- Students who liked the same part of the story pair up and decide why that was their favorite part of the story. They can share their reasons with other partners.
- Students change a part of the story that wasn't their favorite so they like it better. They show or tell how they changed the story.

Variations:

As students become more familiar with Community Circle, there can be three or more circles sharing at the same time.

Other Applications:

- To help students develop an interest in a story, students can draw about their likes and see how they compare with what the characters like. Example: They draw what they had for dinner, share it in Community Circle, and then compare it to what a story character had for dinner.
- Tell all but the ending of a story. Students create endings to share. Then read their story ending.
- Draw the part of the story that made you feel happiest. Be ready to tell why.

Curran's Comments:

For the first few times primary students do Community Circle, it is important that all the students are together in the same circle so the teacher can monitor how well they use Active Listening. When the students can use Active Listening and the Speak Louder signal (see Chapter 2) the class can be divided into two or more circles that are sharing at the same time. An advantage of several circles is that all the students have a chance to share within a shorter time. A disadvantage is that the students and teacher don't have a chance to hear all the ideas that are shared.

Favorite Farm Fauna

• Literature
Family Farm
The Animals of Buttercup Farm
The Big Red Barn
Farming
Midnight Farm
Farm Animal Book

• Grade Level
K-2

• Type of Lesson
Making Choices
Sharing Ideas: Animal Preferences

• Cognitive Objective
Students decide what kind of farm animal they would like to take care and express at least two reasons for their choice.

• Social Skills Objective
Quiet Voices

• Materials
Picture cards to label corners (included), color cards (3"x4" construction paper), a color for each corner, and Post-Its..

Structures
- **Corners**
- **Partner Discussion**
- **Think-Pair-Share**

Background Information

The class has read and discussed several books about farm animals. Some of the stories the students could have heard are: *The Animals of Buttercup Farm* by Phoebe and Judy Dunn, *The Big Red Barn* by Margaret Wise Brown, *Farming* by Gail Gibbons, *Midnight Farm* by Rose Lindbergh, *Farm Animal Book* by Jane Miller.

For this particular lesson the students should have heard the story *Family Farm* by Thomas Locker. Students will have used quiet voices in other lessons so they will know how to talk quietly so they do not disturb other groups.

Lesson Overview

"As the story, Family Farm shows us, many times boys and girls who live on farms have to help with a lot of the work. Today we are going to pretend that we are part of a farm family and need to be responsible for taking care of one of the kinds of animals that live on the farm. Then you will need to think of the reasons why you chose that animal. While we discuss our reasons, we need to use quiet voices so all groups will be able to hear as they have their discussions."

Lesson Sequence

Corners:

Choose Animal to Care For

A. Preparation for Corners
Make sure all students have access to a Post-it or small piece of paper to write

---

down the corner they choose. "Students, I am putting up picture cards in each corner of the room to show you which animals are on our farm. Think about which one you would like to take care of. Write the name of the animal you choose on your Post-it."

B. Go to Corners
"In a minute you will put on your Post-it, then go to the corner of the room where the picture card for your animal. When you get there show Active Listening."

Corners Group Discussion:

Reasons for Choice
"Take a few minutes for the people in your corner to discuss reasons why they chose that particular animal as the one they wanted to take care of. Remember to use quiet voices that can only be heard by the people in your corner." While they are discussing, pass out colored paper cards to each student. Have a different color for each corner group.

Curran's Comments:
If there is a large number of students in any of the corners, divide those students into two separate groups. Four students in each group are plenty. The smaller the groups are, the greater the participation will be.

Finger Evaluation:

Evaluate Quiet Voices
"If you feel your group used quiet voices that could only be heard by the people in

your group, show thumbs up. If you feel the other teams used quiet voices so your team wasn't disturbed during your discussion, show thumbs up. Compliment them for a being considerate of others. If you notice there are groups who feel they were disturbed by other groups talking, discuss what could have helped their group have a quieter place to work."

Partner Discussion:

Share Reasons
"Students, at this time you are to find someone that has a color card that is a different color than your color card. The two of you will become sharing partners and tell each other two reasons for having chosen that animal as the one you would like to care for. Continue to use quiet six inch voices. Watch for my silent signal."

Hand Signal Evaluation:

Sharing Two Reasons
Give the silent signal. "If your partner gave you two reasons for having chosen his/her animal, put your left hand on your head. If you both have a hand on your head, reach out with your right hands and give each other a handshake for a job well done."

Think-Pair-Share:

Debrief the Lesson
Students use Think-Pair-Share to discuss some of the following questions.
* "What made it easy to choose an animal and discuss reasons for choosing that animal with the rest of the people in your corner?"

* "How did you feel about telling a couple of those reasons to your sharing partner?"
* "How did it feel to use quiet voices while you were discussing?"

Extensions:

* Students meet back in their corner groups and form teams of three to five to make animal care books.
* Students pair up with a person who had a different animal and write a story or list of directions to teach the other person everything that must be done to give his/her animal good care.
* Students pretend they get to stay on a farm to take care of their favorite animal. They write a letter to their parents, telling them about their experiences on the farm.
* Make a graph that shows how many students chose each particular animal.

Other Applications:

* Four characters from a story can be the four corners. Students decide on their favorite character, the bravest character, the most important character, or the smartest character.
* The corners could represent four different events from the story. Students could decide which was their favorite event and give their reasons why.
* The corners could represent four different characters from the story. Students could think about one event from the story. Each corner would write a diary entry for their character explaining how their character felt about that event.
* The corners could represent four different stories that contain the same type of animal or character. The groups think of words that describe their particular character. Then groups compare lists of words to see how the characters are the same or different.

SHEEP

COWS

Picture Cards for Favorite Farm Fauna

CHICKENS

PIGS

Prime Time

Lesson 5

• Literature
Jesse Bear, What Will You Wear?

• Grade Level
K-2

• Type of Lesson
Sharing Ideas: Favorite time of day

• Cognitive Objective
Students decide what would be their favorite time of day, decide reasons for their choice, and be ready to share those reasons.

• Social Skills Objective
Active Listening

• Materials
Post-Its or small pieces of paper, Time of the Day Cards.

Structures

- *Class Discussion*
- *Corners*
- *Group Discussion*
- *Partner Discussion*
- *Roundrobin*
- *Teams Share*

Background Information
Students have heard or read the story *Jesse Bear, What Will You Wear?* by Nancy White Carlstrom. They have had opportunities to discuss many types of clothing people wear. Also, they understand the meaning of morning, noon, and evening.

Lesson Overview
"Jesse Bear talked about the different times of day. We are now going to decide which is our favorite time of day and why it is our favorite time of day. We will have a chance to share our ideas with the class. As we work together we want to remember to use all parts of active listening."

Curran's Comments:
If the students are not able to write, use numbers or colors to designate the groups.

Lesson Sequence
Class Discussion:
Reviewing Active Listening
"What things should we remember to do to show that we are active listeners?" The students will probably give responses such as the following: "We should look at the person who is talking." "We should keep our hands to ourselves." "We need to think about what the person is saying."

Corners:
Favorite Time of Day
A. Choose Favorite Time
"Jesse Bear talked about morning, noon, and evening. Think which of these is

---

your favorite time of day. Write your choice on the Post-it that is being passed to you."

B. Form Corners Groups
"I have hung signs, each showing a different time of day. Go to the part of the room with the sign that matches the word on your Post-it." Have Corners groups check that everyone is in the right corner. The groups will probably be large, so break them down into groups of four.

Roundrobin Group Discussion:

Reasons for Favorite Time
Have the students in each group number themselves from one to four. "Students, your group will discuss why you like that particular time of day. After the group members have shared several reasons, have each person in the group practice saying at least two reasons that the group has mentioned so they will be able to share these reasons with someone from another group."

Finger Signal Evaluation:

Use of Active Listening
"In a few seconds, you will give a thumbs up if you think the people in your group used active listening. You will give a thumbs down if you think they forgot. Show your signal.

Roundrobin:

Validation of Signal
Now going around the group in order, first Person #1, then #2, #3, and #4, say one sentence that explains to the group why you showed thumbs up or thumbs down. Teams that had all thumbs up, give yourselves a silent cheer."

Teams Share:

Share Reasons
Put two groups of four together to share the reasons for choosing a particular time of day. It is more interesting if groups from different Corners Groups are put together. "Now that two groups are together, the number ones become partners, the number twos are partners, the number threes are partners, and so are the number fours. Partners, show each other your Post-it that tells the time of day you chose. Then tell two reasons why your group decided it was their favorite time of day. Watch that your partner is an active listener."

Partner Discussion:

Evaluate Active Listening
"Tell your partner how you could tell they were using active listening." Give students a couple of minutes to discuss this. As they do, listen to what the partners are sharing with each other. "Put your Post-it on your shoulder if you could tell your partner that he/she was using active listening." Repeat some of the reasons for active listening that you heard the students telling their partners. Praise or reward according to how many Post-its you see on shoulders.

Group Discussion:

Debrief the Lesson
Find out how the students felt about the lesson by having the sharing groups discuss some of the following questions.
* What made you feel comfortable about sharing reasons for liking a

Lorna Curran: *Lessons for Little Ones: Language Arts*©
Kagan Cooperative Learning • 1 (800) Wee Co-op

time of day with your group and with a partner?

- What made it easy for you to use active listening when your partner was sharing ideas with you?

- What would make it even easier to share next time?

Other Applications:

- Students decide on their favorite day of the week and go to Corners to decide on reasons for it being their favorite.

- Students decide on their favorite month and go to corners groups to share reasons.

- Students decide upon their favorite holiday and go to corners groups to share reasons.

- Students decide on their favorite story character, and discuss in corners why that character was their favorite.

- Students decide which is their favorite story and discuss why that story was their favorite.

Extensions:

- Students can make a poster showing and describing their favorite thing they do at that time of day.

- Students could make a time of day book where they have a chapter for morning, a chapter for noon, and a chapter for evening. In each chapter they show and tell about things they do. To extend into math, clock faces showing the exact time can be added.

Time of the Day Cards

Morning

Noon

Evening

Lorna Curran: *Lessons for Little Ones: Language Arts*©
Kagan Cooperative Learning • 1 (800) Wee Co-op

Beary Good or Beary Bad

• Literature

Goldilocks and the Three Bears

• Grade Level

K-2

• Type of Lesson

Establishing Values: Agree/Disagree with a character's behavior

• Cognitive Objective

Students decide whether or not a character's actions were appropriate and establish reasons for the answer they chose.

• Social Skills Objective

Paraphrasing

• Materials

A yarn or tape line, Post-Its or small pieces of paper, and strips of three different colors.

• Line-Ups
• Inside-Outside Circle
• Partner Discussion

Structures

Background Information

Students have heard or read the story *Goldilocks and the Three Bears*.

Lesson Overview

"Today we are going to think about things that happened in the story Goldilocks and the Three Bears. We shall see how we feel about those events. We will stand on a Line-Up to show how we feel. Then we will tell our partners the reasons we chose our answer and they will paraphrase our answer back so we can tell if they understood us."

Lesson Sequence

Line-Ups:

Share Opinions about Characters

A. Preparation for Line-Ups

The teacher lays out a yarn or tape that is long enough for the class to stand on.

Students are given Post-its or small papers so they can write their answer choice.

B. Class Discussion: Practice Paraphrasing

"Students, we are going to paraphrase which is listening to what a person says and then, using slightly different words, tell them what they said. Let's take a minute and practice paraphrasing before we start the lesson. Be ready to paraphrase this sentence: 'Paraphrasing is using almost the same words to tell someone what you heard them say.'" Call on a couple of students to share how they would paraphrase the sentence. (Kindergarten students have more success if they only repeat what they heard.)

C. Make the Statement

"Students, you are to decide if it was all right for Goldilocks to go inside the Three Bears' house while they were gone."

Lorna Curran: *Lessons for Little Ones: Language Arts*©
Kagan Cooperative Learning • 1 (800) Wee Co-op   **Lesson 6: 1**

D. Students Write Their Answer

"If you feel it was all right, write a 'yes' on your small paper. If you feel it was not all right, write a 'no' on your paper. If you are not sure if Goldilocks should have gone in or not, write 'maybe.'"

E. Students Show Answers in a Line-Up

"Students, take your answer paper and a Line-Up by the word you chose."

F. Group Discussion: Reasons for Answer Choice

After the students have arranged themselves in a Line-Up, give each group a question to discuss.

- The "yes" group - Why was it all right for Goldilocks to enter the bears' house?
- The "maybe" group - Why can't you be sure it was all right for Goldilocks to enter the bears' house?
- The "no" group - Why wasn't it all right for Goldilocks to enter the bears' house?

G. Group Identification Strips

While the groups discuss their reasons, pass out colored strips of paper to each student. Use a different color for each group.

Partner Discussion:

Paraphrase Statements

Give the students a minute to find a partner within their group. "Students signal to me who your partner is by giving the hitch hiking signal towards your partner. One of you is to tell one of the reasons your group discussed about Goldilocks entering the bear's house. The other person is to paraphrase what you said. Then

the opposite partners shares a reason and paraphrase what was said."

Finger Signal Evaluation:

Use of Paraphrasing

Students show thumbs up to signal that their partners did paraphrase what they said.

Partner Discussion:

Share Reasons

"Students, each of the groups, 'yes', 'maybe', and 'no,' have been given different color paper strips. In a moment, you will find someone who has a strip that is a different color than your strip. This person will have a different idea than you do. So be a good listener so you will be able to paraphrase their ideas back to them. Start with one of you sharing how you feel about Goldilocks going into the bears' house and your reason for that answer. The other person paraphrases the reason. Then switch jobs and share and paraphrase again. "

Curran's Comments:

Having different color strips for each of the opinion groups, "yes," "no," and "maybe," makes it easy for students to find a partner who has a different opinion. Students can change partners several times. Each time they try to find a partner with a new color so they hear a new opinion.

Finger Signal Evaluation:

Use of Paraphrasing

Again, students show thumbs up to signal that their partners did paraphrase what they said.

Inside-Outside Circle:

Debrief the Team

Have the partners form an Inside-Outside Circle to discuss the questions to find out how the students felt about working together to do this lesson. They could rotate to several people as each question is asked so they can hear different opinions.

- What did you enjoy about doing the Line-Up?
- What was hard or easy about sharing reasons in your group or with a partner?
- What made paraphrasing easy or hard for you?

Other Applications:

- *Cinderella* by Paul Galdone: Was it all right for Cinderella to go to the Ball?
- *Clifford the Big Red Dog* by Norman Bridwell: Would Clifford be a good pet for you?
- *Fredreck* by Leo Lionni: Was it all right for Fredreck to store up words while the other mice worked storing up food?
- *Ira Sleeps Over* by Bernard Waber: Is it all right to be afraid on a dark night? Is it all right to take a security item with you?
- *Crow Boy* by Taro Yashima: Does everyone need to act the same? Feel the same?

Extensions:

- Students who felt it was all right for Goldilocks to go into the bears' house, write an ending for the story where they use their reasons to have Goldilocks explain to her mother why it was OK for her to go to the bears' house.
- The students who felt Golidlocks shouldn't go into the bears' house, use their reasons to write an ending to the story where Goldilock's mother explains why Goldilocks should never go there again. The maybe group could make up a list that tells all the good things about Goldilocks' visit to the bears house and all the bad things about the visit. The students could discuss and write if they think their reasons would stay the same or change if Baby Bear were to visit Goldilock's house.
- Have the students pretend they are Goldilocks and explain why she went into the three bears' house.
- Have the students discuss and share what the three bears and Goldilocks should do differently next time.
- Read the letter from Goldilocks in the book *The Jolly Postman* by Janet and Allan Ahlberg. The students could write a response to Goldilocks.

Variations:

Other questions to use for this story are:
- Should the three bears have left their house unlocked?
- Should Goldilocks have eaten the three bears' food?
- Should Goldilocks have used the three bears' furniture?
- Should Goldilocks have run away?

A Good Friend for Me

Lesson 7

• Literature
Frog & Toad Are Friends

• Grade Level
1-2

• Type of Lesson
Establishing Values: What makes a good friend

• Cognitive Objective
Students think of reasons why or why not character from a story would have right characteristics to be good friend.

• Social Skills Objective
Active Listening

• Materials
Post-Its or small pieces of paper for making their answers, yarn or tape for the line, and pencils.

Structures
• **Class Discussion**
• **Line-Ups**
• **Partner Discussion**
• **Think-Pair-Share**

Background Information
The students have explored different books about friends and friendship. They have talked about what makes a good friend. The students have read enough of a story to become familiar with the characteristics of one of the characters in the story. Some suggested titles are: *Frog & Toad Are Friends* by Arnold Lobel; *Who Will Be My Friends?* by Syd Hoff; *Will I Have A Friend?* by Miriam Cohen; and *Do You Want to Be My Friend?* by Eric Carle.

Lesson Overview
"Students, we are going to do a Line-Up that shows if we think a certain story book character would or would not be a good friend for us. We will need to use Active Listening as we discuss the reasons for choosing our answers."

Lesson Sequence
Line-Ups:
Story Character for a Friend
A. Preparing for the Line-Up
The teacher lays out a yarn or tape long enough for the class to stand on for the Line-Up. Each student is given a supply of Post-its.

B. Marking an Answer
"I am going to mention the name of a character from the story. You are to think if this character would or would not make a good friend. Then think of some reasons why this character would or would not make a good friend. If you think the character would make a good friend for you, write the word 'yes' on your Post-it. If you think the character would not make a good friend, mark it

'no.' If you are not sure if this character would be a good friend, write, 'maybe.'"

C. Make the Line Up
"Put on your Post-it. Come stand on the Line-Up. If you feel the character would be an excellent friend, stand at the end of the line that is labeled 'good.' If you feel the character would be just a fairly good friend, stand more towards the middle of the line. If you feel the character would be a bad friend, go all the way to the end to show that the character would be a bad friend for you to have; be a little more towards the middle if you feel it might be just a little bit bad to have this character for a friend."

Partner Discussion:
Describe and Practice Active Listening
Have the students number themselves one, two, one, two along the Line-Up. Have the ones stand on one side of the line and the twos on the other side. Ones and twos face each other, forming partners. "For the next two parts of the Line-Up it is important to use Active Listening so we can hear and think about the answers that are shared. First, partners will be sharing answers with each other, and then, the whole class will be sharing answers. Remember the important parts of Active Listening and quietly tell them to your partner. First, partner #1 will tell a reason, then, partner #2 will tell a reason. You may alternate telling reasons until time is called in a couple of minutes." Then listen as the other person tells you the parts of Active Listening." Walk along the Line-Up as they discuss the important components of Active Listening. Reinforce the correct definition of Active Listening by complimenting them for saying things such as: "You should look at the person who is speaking." "You should be listening instead of talking." "You should think about what the person is saying." "Keep your hands to yourself." Write these statements down as you share them with the class so they can be used for evaluation of Active Listening throughout the lesson.

Finger Evaluation:
Use of Active Listening
"Listen as I read our list of Active Listening suggestions. Be ready to show how many of these suggestions we followed." Read the list, count to three, say "Show" and the students will signal their answers by raising the correct number of fingers to indicate how many of the suggestions they thought were followed. Record how many voted for each number. Ask for a couple of suggestions on how the class could improve their Active Listening.

Partner Discussion:
Reasons for Student's Positions in the Line-Up
"Partners, we are going to find out the reasons for this character being a good or bad friend. Remember, first partner #1 will tell a reason, then partner #2 will tell a reason. You may continue telling reasons until time is called."

Think-Pair-Share:
Evaluate Active Listening
Give partners time to think to themselves about the things they did to use active listening. Then they discuss in pairs how they used Active Listening. After they have had a couple of minutes to discuss,

provide the students time to share answers with the class.

Class Discussion:

Share the Reason

"Now we will list the reasons for the character being a good or bad friend. Raise your hand if you would like to share a reason you or your partner said. When all your reasons have been given, go to your seat." Call on students and list the reasons until everyone's ideas have been recorded.

Think-Pair-Share:

Evaluate Active Listening

Repeat the evaluation process. Notice if the vote showed improvement. Compliment and/or reward the improvement. Have the students discuss with their partners the things the class did best as they used Active Listening. Repeat some of the positive comments you hear. Praise and/or reward accordingly.

Class Discussion:

Analyze the Results of the Line-Up

"Students, before we go to our seats look at our Line-Up. Think what this line-up shows us about what kind of friend this character would be." Ask for student responses. Record their thoughts.

Partner Discussion:

Debrief the Lesson

Have the partners discuss these questions to see how they felt about doing the line-up.

- What made the line-up easy and fun for you to do?

- What would make it even easier to do next time?

Variations:

If the students have a difficult time standing on the Line-Up while ideas are listed, they could:

- Sit down along the Line-Up.
- Go to their seats and share from there.
- Go to their teams and compile reasons to be shared with other groups.
- Make individual lists of reasons they and their partner discussed. These lists can be passed several times so students can read each other's lists.

Extensions:

- Use the list of reasons for the story character being a good friend, to write a descriptive paragraph about why they would like the character as a friend.
- Use the list of reasons for being a good friend to create a poster advertising for a new friend that would have certain qualities.
- The students write an advertisement asking for a new friend in which they would list their own qualities that would make them be a good friend.
- Make good and bad friends lists for several story characters and then compare the similarities and differences between the qualities of the two characters.
- Each of the teams can make a chart that tells one or more good friend qualities for each member of the team. This activity can also be done for each member of the class.

Fortunately/ Unfortunately

• Literature

Fortunately/Unfortunately

• Grade Level
1-2

• Type of Lesson
Establishing Values: What is fortunate and unfortunate

• Cognitive Objective
Students stand in Line-Up to express how they feel about about a situation, then use results of Line-Up to make fortunately or unfortunately statements to use for a story.

• Social Skills Objective
Quiet Voices

• Materials
Yarn or tape for a line, paper markers labeled good, so-so, bad, to indicate positions on line, post-its or small paper for expressing opinions, large drawing paper to make the Fortunately/Unfortunately books.

Structures
- *Class Discussion*
- *Line-Ups*
- *Partners*
- *Partner Discussion*

Background Information

The students have heard or read the story *Fortunately/Unfortunately* by Remy Charlip. They will have discussed some situations that are fortunate situations and some that are unfortunate situations.

Lesson Overview

"Students, you will have a chance to express whether a situation would be a fortunate or unfortunate situation and make a Line-Up. While we are on the Line-Up we are to use quiet voices. You then will use the ideas from our Line-Up to create a fortunately/unfortunately book."

Lesson Sequence

Line-Ups

Show Feelings about Situations

A. Mark the Line
The teacher lays out a yarn or tape line labeled "good" at one end, "so-so" in the middle, and "bad" on the other end.

B. Describe Situation
The teacher describes a situation and the students decide how they feel about that situation. A sample situation could be: "Mother will serve chocolate cake for dinner."

C. Students Record Their Feelings
The students are given a supply of Post-its to record their answers. They write the word "good" on their Post-it if they

feel it is a good situation. They write the word "bad" on their Post-it if they feel it is not a good situation. They write "so-so" if they are not sure whether it is a good or a bad situation.

D. Students Show Their Answer in the Line-Up

The students are given the following directions. "In a moment, you will bring your Post-it and stand by the label that matches the word on your Post-it. If you feel it is a very good situation, you will stand all the way over to the end of the line by the word 'good.' If you feel the situation is just a little bit good, you will stand between the words 'good' and 'so-so.' You will do the same thing at the end of the line labeled 'bad.' Your second job is to use quiet voices while you are finding your place in the Line-Up. We will evaluate how well we did this after we have made our Line-Up."

Class Discussion:

Analyze Results of the Line-Up
Form Fortunately/Unfortunately Statements

Direct the students to look at the Line-Up to see where most of the students are standing. Have them decide, whether the Line-Up shows them it is a good or a bad situation. If most of the students are on the 'good' end of the Line-Up, it is a situation that can be described by using the word fortunately. The students will join you in saying the statement, "Fortunately, Mother will serve chocolate cake for dessert."

Finger Evaluation:

Use of Quiet Voices

Students are asked to think about the type of voices they heard around them.

When the teacher says, "One, two, three, show," they will hold up five fingers if all the voices they heard were quiet voices. They will hold up three fingers if some of the voices were quiet and some were not. They will hold up one finger if most of the voices they heard were too loud. The teacher gives the signal and the students show the appropriate number of fingers. Call on a few students. Ask them their reasons for their answer. Look to see which number is most frequent. Ask a few students for reasons why the class did so well and for ways the class could do even better.

Line-Ups:

Discover More Fortunately/Unfortunately Situations

Repeat the Line-Up to discover how the class feels about some other situations and then use the results of the Line-Up to make fortunately/unfortunately statements.

Other statements to make are:
- "When Mother went to the freezer it was empty." (unfortunately)
- "Father went to the store to get some ice cream." (fortunately)
- "All the store had was mint ice cream." (could go either way)

After they do each Line-Up, have them evaluate how well they did in using quiet voices. Keep track of any improvement in the number of students that feel the class is doing a perfect job.

Partners:

Create Fortunately/Unfortunately Books

Students work in pairs to think of good and bad situations that can be made into fortunately/unfortunately statements. They illustrate the statements and make them into a book to share with the class. For example, using the statements above, one partner would draw a picture of mother at the empty freezer and write the unfortunate statement on the picture while the other partner draws a picture of father at the store getting more ice cream and would write the fortunate statement on this picture. They can continue thinking of unfortunate and fortunate statements to illustrate that would continue their story.

Line-Ups:

Check Accuracy of Student Books

The fortunately/unfortunately statements made in the student books can be acted out by doing a line-up to see if the class has the same feelings about the situations as the student authors did.

Class Discussion:

Evaluation of Quiet Voices

Have the students think if they followed the suggestions for using quiet voices as they did the line-up. Did they recall seeing more people showing five fingers each time they evaluated? Doing a perfect job or showing improvement can be rewarded with compliments, points, coupons, etc.

Partner Discussion:

Debrief the Lesson

Partners discuss the following questions to see how the students felt about doing the line-up.

- What made it easy or hard for you to decide on an answer to the questions?
- What made the line-up fun?
- What is something you learned as you did the line-up?
- How did it feel to have others make suggestions on how to improve?
- How did it feel when you tried to use the suggestions?
- What made it easy to work with your partner to make the book?
- What could make it even easier next time?
- How did you feel when the class was acting out your book?
- How did it feel to act out books from other groups?

Variations:

Other situations to change to fortunately/unfortunately statements:

Situation #1

- You get to watch a game on TV.
- Dad says he would like to get tickets and take you to a game.
- The tickets cost $50.00 each.
- Your family just won the lottery.

Situation #2

- You forgot to do your homework.
- Tomorrow is Saturday.
- The family will go away all day Sunday.
- Monday is a holiday.

Reliving Rapunzel

Lesson 9

• Literature
Rapunzel

• Grade Level
1-3

• Type of Lesson
Establishing Values: Agree/Disagree with character's behavior, expressing values through role play

• Cognitive Objective
Students will learn people differ in reactions to story characters, discover reasons for character's behavior, and role play character.

• Social Skills Objective
Active Listening, everyone participates, accepting opinions politely

• Materials
Post-Its or small pieces of paper, yarn, tape, lined paper, and cards labeled yes, no, maybe.

Structures
- **Cooperative Project**
- **Group Discussion**
- **Line-Ups**
- **Numbered Heads**
- **Partners**
- **Roundtable**
- **Team Interview**
- **Teams Share**

Background Information
The students have heard or read the story *Rapunzel* by Barbara Rogasky.

Lesson Overview
Overview of Lesson
"We shall use a line-up to find out how we feel about things characters did in the story Rapunzel. Then you will think of questions you would like to ask the story characters to find out why they behaved the way they did. Finally you will have a chance to pretend you are one of the story characters so you can give reasons for why a character acted as he or she did."

Lesson Sequence
Line-Ups:
Show Reaction to Story Character
A. Explain the Line-Up
"In a few minutes I will be <u>asking you a question</u> about what a character in the story did. You should <u>think about the question</u> for a minute, <u>choose your answer, write your answer</u> on a Post-it, and <u>decide what your reasons were</u> for choosing that answer." Write the underlined words on the board as you give directions so they will remember the procedure for selecting an answer. "Then you will stand on this yarn line I am laying down. You will stand at this end of the line if your answer is 'Yes,' at that end if your answer is 'No,' and in the middle if your answer is 'Maybe.'"

B. Class Discussion: Examples of Polite Statements

"While you are on the line, you will be sharing your reasons for your opinion and listening to other students reasons for their opinions. You are to do this in a polite way." Have the students give examples of things they could do or say to be polite. Examples might be: Things to do: Show Active Listening. Nod your head. Face your partner. Things to say: Good idea. I wouldn't have thought of that. That's an interesting idea.

C. Make a Choice

"In the story, Rapunzel's father went into the witch's garden to get rampion. Do you think the father should have gone into the witch's garden to get rampion? Think what your answer will be; 'Yes,' 'No,' or 'Maybe.' Write your answer on your Post-it."

Yes	_Maybe_	_No_

D. Do the Line-Up

When the students have finished writing their answer, announce that it is time for them to put on the Post-it and line up by the card that matches their Post-it.

Partners Discuss:

Discovering Similar Opinions

Show the silent signal. Give directions for the students to number off one, two, one, two, along the line. The ones will all

Lines of Ones	XXXXXXXXXX
Lines of Twos	XXXXXXXXXX

stand on one side of the line and the twos will stand on the other side of the line. The ones and twos will pair up along the line to become discussion partners. They will be given a couple of minutes to share reasons they had for making their choice. Remind them of how they can act politely. After they have shared, ask them if they noticed any new ways of being polite that should be added to the Class Chart.

Line-Ups — Split and Slide:

Discovering Different Opinions

Tell the students that they will be sharing their reasons with a new partner. This time they must remember something their partner does to be polite. Have the students stand back in one line. Split the line in the middle. Have half the line take a step forward so the students are in two lines. Have one line move to the far end of the other line so it is now a double line with the "yes" students facing half of the "maybe" students and half the "maybe" students facing the "no" students. The students face their new partner who is standing in the line opposite them. They share their reasons as before. When they have finished sharing, direct them to return to their seats.

Partners:

Recognition of Polite Statements

On a Post-it, the students write down something positive that their partner said or did. These can be displayed on a Cooperative Learning Bulletin Board.

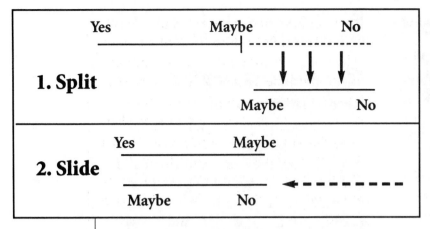

1. Split	Yes — Maybe ⊣ - - - - - No
	Maybe No (↓ ↓ ↓)
2. Slide	Yes ——— Maybe
	Maybe No ← - - - - -

Recognition of Different Opinions

Give the students a few minutes to write down their own opinion and a reason for having that opinion. Then they are to write down a different opinion and that person's reason for having that opinion. Use the information on the slips to validate that they are aware of different opinions on an issue and also that they are aware there can be more than one reason for having an opinion.

Discovering Additional Opinions

Repeat the Line-Up and discussions to discover how the students feel about other events in the story. Other events to consider could be:

- Should the witch have taken Rapunzel?
- Would you have hidden Rapunzel like the witch did?
- Should Rapunzel and the Prince have gone to the Prince's Kingdom?

Roundtable:

Create Questions asked by Characters

"In a few minutes your team will have a chance to brainstorm some questions that the characters in the story might have liked to ask each other so they could find our why they acted as they did in the story." Some ideas could be:

- Rapunzel might like to ask the witch some questions after she was taken to the tower.
- The Prince might like to ask Rapunzel some questions when he found her in the tower.
- Rapunzel might like to ask the Prince some questions when she found him wandering in the forest.
- The wife might like to ask her husband some questions when she found out he had gone into the witch's garden to get rampion.

"As your team thinks of answers, rotate the Brainstorm Sheet so everyone has a chance to record at least one of the questions the team creates. When we are done we will evaluate if all team members participated."

Numbered Heads Together:

Share Questions

When it appears all teams have had enough time to record at least one question, call for Active Listening. Use Numbered Heads Together to have the teams share their questions. Team members number off, then the teacher calls a number. The person with that number will be the person to share one of the team questions. Make a class list of the questions as they are being shared. Check the Group Brainstorm Sheet to see that everyone participated. Praise and/or reward accordingly.

Cooperative Project:
Create Answers for the Questions

"Now your team will look at the list of questions to ask the characters. Think of answers the characters would give to the question and their reasons for answering in that way. Again everyone is to participate. I will pass out an Encourager Card to a person on each team. That person will encourage everyone to participate."

Evaluate Participation

After about 15 minutes, call for Active Listening. Check with the encouragers to see if everyone on the team suggested answers for the questions.

Team Interviews:
Question the Characters

"Now we will have a chance to interview characters from the story to find out why they behaved as they did in the story. Each team is to choose someone to be Rapunzel, the Prince, the witch, the husband, or the wife. I will put two teams together for an interview. I will label the teams as either an 'A' team or a 'B' team. The 'A' team members will be interviewed by the 'B' teammembers first. The 'B' teammembers may ask questions of each character for two minutes. I will be your timekeeper and let you know when it is time to interview the next character. Then I will signal that it is time to switch. Then the 'B' teammembers will be interviewed by the 'A' teammembers. Have your team ask at least one question of each character. If you are not sure what questions to ask, refer to the class list of questions. If a character has a hard time answering a question, the team can huddle and suggest an answer. Be aware of evidence of Active Listening so you will know how to evaluate at the end of the lesson."

Cooperative Project:
Record Interview Information

Now the teams meet as individual teams. They choose a recorder and write down information they received during the interview. They are to read over the sheet carefully, so anyone from the team is ready to share the information with other students.

Group Discussion:
Validate Active Listening

The teams share specific examples, from their team that will validate that their team members used active listening.

Teams Share:
Team Interview Information

Two different teams meet together to share the information they gained during the interview.

Group Discussion:
Debrief the Lesson

Ask the teams some of the following questions to find out how they felt about working together to do this lesson.
- What was easy/hard about finding your place in the Line-Up and sharing your opinion?
- What worked best for your team while you created questions to ask the characters?

Yes	Maybe
No	Maybe

- What was easy/hard about being interviewed by the other team?
- Was there anything that made it easy to interview the other team?

Variations:

- The students can do the wrap when one end of the Line-Up meets the other end of the Line-Up. In this configuration, students with opposite opinions talk with each other.

Interview information can be shared by:
- Calling on a team member to share the information with the class.
- Choosing a team member to go to another team to read the information.
- Passing the sheets from one team to another to be read.
- Collecting the sheets to be displayed.

Extensions:

After going through this series of activities, the students could write a different version of the story from the viewpoint of one of the characters.

- A news article about one of the characters could be done using the information gathered. A more extensive interview may be needed before the article could be completed.
- The interview information could be used to write a diary for one of the characters.
- Two students each assume the role of a different character and record a conversation the two characters might have.
- The students compose letters written to Dear Abby by either the witch, or the husband.

A Happy Birthday for Moon

Lesson 10

• Literature

Happy Birthday, Moon

• Grade Level

K-1

• Type of Lesson

Develop Oral Langauge: Create a Story from a Story

• Cognitive Objective

Students contribute to an idea to create new birthday stories for Moon.

• Social Skills Objective

Active Listening, Happy Talk

• Materials

Large paper for brainstorm sheets, pictures to identify expert groups (included), small papers for individual pictures, large background paper for the new version of the story, crayons or markers and glue.

Structures

- *Class Discussion*
- *Jigsaw/Expert Group*
- *Group Discussion*
- *Cooperative Project*
- *Teams Share*

Background Information

The students have discussed the things they like about birthdays. They have heard the story *Happy Birthday, Moon* by Frank Asch. They have discussed possible answers to these questions.

- What did Bear do for Moon?
- Did Moon really talk to Bear?
- What is an echo?

Lesson Overview

"Class, we have have been reading and discussing the story Happy Birthday, Moon. Today we are going to make our own versions of the story. While we work together in our groups to create the story, we will decide what kinds of Happy Talk statements we can make about our team members' contributions. When we share our stories with each other we will practice using our Active Listening so everyone will have a chance to enjoy the new stories. We will prepare for our story writing by brainstorming ideas to use in the new stories. Then we will meet in our teams to decide who goes to each expert group to get information needed to make our books, and finally meet in our teams to put the new story together."

Lesson Sequence

Class Discussion:

List Happy Talk Statements

Before the expert groups start working, remind them they are to use Happy Talk as they gather ideas for their brainstorm sheet. Give them a minute to discuss possible Happy Talk statements that would be appropriate for this lesson. Have the students volunteer suggestions as you list their ideas.

Jigsaw/Expert Group:

Create New Birthday Stories for Moon

A. Class Discussion: Brainstorm Sample Ideas for Jigsaw/Expert Groups

As a total class, brainstorm a few ideas for each of these topics:

- Types of hats Bear could have had for Moon.
- Other presents Bear could give to Moon.
- Kinds of birthday cakes Moon would like.
- Other places to have Moon's birthday party.

Have a large sheet of paper for each of the categories labeled with pictures of the hat, present, birthday cake and house just like the teams have in their envelopes. As the students suggest ideas, draw a pictorial representation of their idea on the appropriate sheet.

B. Team Members Assigned Corners

The students meet in teams of four. The teams are told that they will make and tell a new version of Happy Birthday Moon. First they will go to expert groups so each team member can come back with a new idea for their team story. Each team receives an envelope which contains four of the provided pictures: a hat, a present, a birthday cake, and a house. Each team member selects one picture. The pictures indicate the expert groups each member goes to.

C. Formation of Expert Groups

Hang the brainstorming papers in different corners of the room to indicate where the expert groups will meet. Direct the students to look at the picture they chose, go to the area where that group will meet, and show active listening when all members of the expert group have arrived.

Group Discussion:

Expert Groups Brainstorm Sheet

Expert groups are given crayons and gather ideas for their topic. As a student contributes a new idea, he/she draws the item on the Brainstorm Sheet. For example: hats: cowboy, baseball, straw, football, fireman, policeman, chef. The teacher moves from group to group listening for Happy Talk. After students have worked for two or three minutes, raise your hand for the silent signal. When the students have all signaled back, have them think about and share some of the Happy Talk their group used. You can share any statement you heard such as, "I know group three was using Happy Talk because I heard someone in that group say, "Good, that's an ideas we don't have yet." I heard many groups saying, "Good idea." Encourage students to use these and other positive statements as they continue their work. The groups continue to gather ideas until there are at least enough ideas so that each member of the group can choose a different item.

Group Project:

Expert Groups Draw

When the expert group is through brainstorming and everyone has chosen an idea to draw, everyone in the group raises their hand. The teacher checks to see that everyone in the hat group has a different type of hat to draw. Each group member draws the individual picture he will take back to his team. Remind the students to continue exchanging Happy Talk as they make their drawings. The group members again check to see that each object or place in the group is different. The teacher or a helper can go to the groups while they are working and write a descriptive sentence. Example: Bear has a cowboy hat for Moon.

Cooperative Project:

Teams Create/Practice New Stories

The students go back to their teams. Each member shares what they made at the expert group. The groups put their pictures together to make a new story about Moon's birthday. The pictures can be arranged in this order: place, hat, present, cake. The students are then ready to practice telling their story for the class or to share the pictures with the class while the teacher and/or the whole class tells the story. The stories might go something like this: Bear had a birthday party for Moon at Disneyland. Bear gave Moon a cowboy hat to wear and a lasso to play with. At the end of the party they had a huge birthday cake shaped like Magic Mountain.

Teams Share:

Tell New Birthday Stories

Completion of the cognitive objective becomes apparent as the teams meet in pairs to share their stories with each other. They should be reminded to use Active Listening as the teams are sharing. Have them notice the things their team does to be good Active Listeners.

Group Discussion:

Evaluation Active Listening

Have the teams discuss how well they think they did in using Active Listening. Have them vote on how well they think their group did. Five fingers means everyone did excellent Active Listening. Three fingers means they did Active Listening most of the time. One finger means that their group forgot to use Active Listening this time. Have them show the apropriate number of fingers to represent their vote when they hear the command, "One, Two, Three, Show." Ask several or all the groups to give you a specific reason why they had that number.

Class Discussion:

Recall Happy Talk

Have the students think about the Happy Talk they used while they were in their teams. See if there are any more Happy Talk statements they can add to the Happy Talk list.

Class Discussion:

Debrief the Lesson

Have the students discuss how it felt to have a group to work with when they were gathering ideas for the story.

* How did it feel when you went back to your group and put all the pictures together to make a story?

Other Titles:

Suggested titles about finding birthday presents:
* *Ask Mr. Bear* by Marjorie Flack
* *Mr. Rabbit and the Lovely Surprise* by Charlotte Zolotow

Pictures for Happy Birthday Moon

Lorna Curran: *Lessons for Little Ones: Language Arts*©
Kagan Cooperative Learning • 1 (800) Wee Co-op

Lesson 10:4

Recite A Rhyme

Lesson 11

• Literature

Tomie dePaola's Mother Goose
by Tomie dePaola

• Grade Level

K-2

• Type of Lesson

Developing Oral Language:
Recitation of a rhyme with
simultaneous recording

• Cognitive Objective

Students tell a Mother Goose rhyme to a
small group of students.

• Social Skills Objective

Strong Voices

• Materials

An illustration or title sheet of the rhyme for each team, sequence recording sheets -
three per team, large paper for illustrating the rhyme when teams finish, "Excellent Speaker"
coupons (included), Rountable Sequence Board.

Structures

- **Cooperative Project**
- **Group Discussion**
- **Roundrobin**

Background Information

The students have heard or read a rhyme until they are familiar enough with it so that most of the students know most of the rhyme.

Lesson Overview

"The teams will give everyone a chance to say todays' rhyme. One member at a time will say the rhyme while the others record that all parts of the rhyme that were said. The person saying the rhyme will need to speak clearly so the rest of the team can hear."

Lesson Sequence
Roundrobin:

Learn A Rhyme
A. Set Up Groups
Arrange the students in groups of four, making sure there is at least one student in each group who knows the rhyme perfectly and so there is one student who could use some help learning the rhyme. Give them a few minutes to practice saying the rhyme together as a team.

B. Model Roundrobin Storytelling
Choose three students to join you in modeling Roundrobin storytelling.

C. Preparation for Roundrobin
The students are numbered off from one to four. Have them sit by their number on the Roundtable Sequence Board. Person #1 is given a sheet with an illustra-

tion or the title of the rhyme to be recited. Members #2, #3, and #4 are given Sequence Recording Sheets which illustrate the main events in the rhyme. (see samples on pages 11:5 & 11:6). Each team member selects a different color crayon to be used when it is their turn to circle the items pictured on the Sequence Recording Sheet.

Roundrobin Team Practice:

Rhyme Recitation

To begin the recitations, person #1 recites the rhyme. At the same time, the other team members circle each item pictured in box #1 as person #1 mentions it while telling the rhyme.

Team Evaluation:

Excellent Speaker Coupons

When person #1 finishes reciting the rhyme, the other team members decide if they could easily hear the rhyme as it was told. Each team member who could hear, gives person #1 an Excellent Speaker Coupon.

Roundrobin Team Practice:

Complete the Rhyme Recitation

Everyone then passes the papers to the person on their left. Now person #2 has the illustration and recites the rhyme while team members #1, #3, and #4 circle the items that are said in box # 2 of the recording sheet that was passed to them. The groups continue reciting, recording and passing until all the group members have recited the rhyme and the group has recorded the events they included in their recitation.

Team Practice:

The Rhyme

If any team member had difficulty saying the rhyme, the team only circles the items the person could remember. When everyone has had their turn, the team should practice saying the rhyme several times until all the team members know it very well. Pass the picture/title sheet to the person who will be retelling the rhyme and the recording sheets to the rest of the team. Again circle the items on the recording sheet as this person retells the rhyme. Repeat this process until all team members can tell the whole rhyme correctly.

Cooperative Project:

Illustration of the Rhyme

"If everyone on your team tells the rhyme correctly before the time is up, the team can make their own illustration of the rhyme."

Recognition of Excellent Speaking

The groups evaluate how well they did in using a speaking voice that could be heard by all group members by counting up the excellent speaker coupons. All groups that have 12 to 16 coupons are rewarded (praise, cheers, certificates, or points).

Group Discussion:

Debrief the Lesson

Debrief by discussing in teams and then as a class, some or all of the following:
* What made it easy to record as the team members said the rhyme? Why or why not?

- How did it feel to get "Excellent Speaker" coupons?
- What did your team do to make it easy for each person to say the rhyme?

Extensions:

- Students are now ready to tell the rhyme to their parents or to other classes.
- Teams could create a new version of the rhyme by changing characters, locations, or events. They then go through the same process to memorize the new rhyme.
- Teams could exchange their rhymes and memorize another team's rhyme.

Other Applications:

- Use the procedure to share poems.
- Use the procedure to tell short stories.

Curran's Comments:

The Roundtable Sequence Board is a large circle which is traced and cut out of tag board. It is marked with the numbers one to four which indicates the sequence of turns. It is also marked with arrows which indicate the direction the sequence recording sheets are being passed.

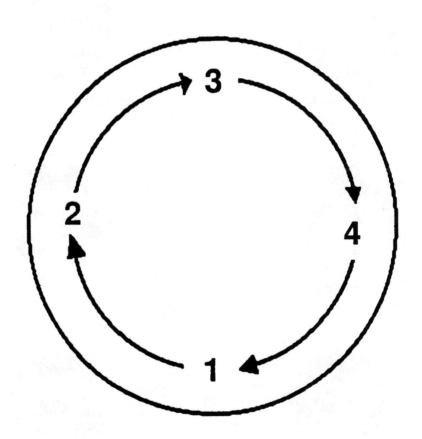

Roundtable Sequence Board

Excellent Speaker Coupons

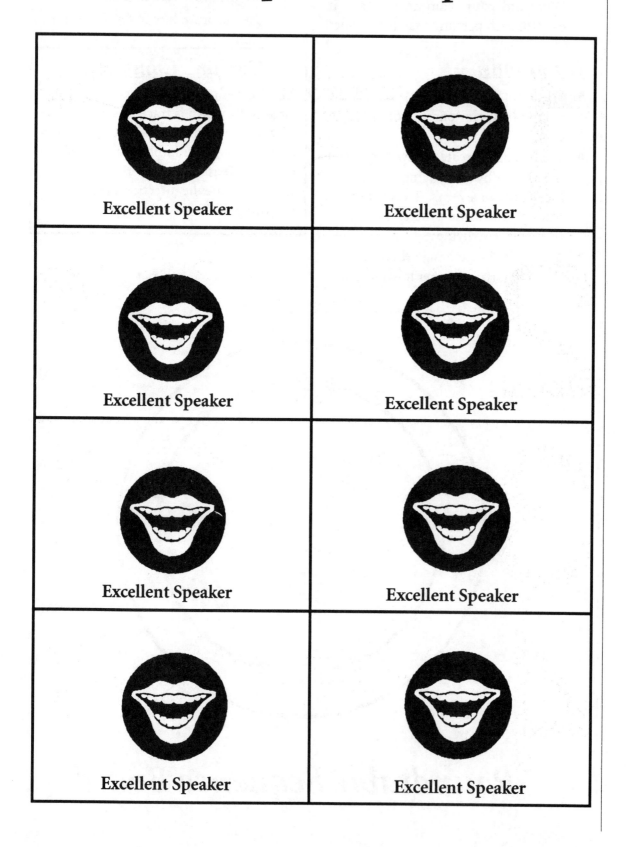

Lorna Curran: *Lessons for Little Ones: Language Arts*©
Kagan Cooperative Learning • 1 (800) Wee Co-op

Sequence Recording Sheet

Lorna Curran: *Lessons for Little Ones: Language Arts*©
Kagan Cooperative Learning • 1 (800) Wee Co-op   **Lesson 11:5**

Sequence Recording Sheet

Humpty Dumpty

Lorna Curran: *Lessons for Little Ones: Language Arts*©

Kagan Cooperative Learning • 1 (800) Wee Co-op

Sense-a-Tional Stories

• Literature
Frederick
Who's Hiding Here
Animalia

• Grade Level
K-2

• Type of Lesson
Develop Oral Language: Story Writing/ Descriptive Words

• Cognitive Objective
Groups create a story from a set of pictures, using descriptive words for each object in the story.

• Social Skills Objective
Everyone Participates

• Materials
Large paper for the expert group brainstorm sheets, large paper for the team illustrations, pencils, crayons, and glue, pictures for each of the categories.

Structures
• **Cooperative Project**
• **Jigsaw/Expert Groups**
• **Inside-Outside Circle**
• **Group Discussion**

Background Information
Students have heard stories that are rich in descriptive words such as *Frederick* by Leo Lionni, *Who's Hiding Here* by Yoshi, and *Animalia* by Graeme Base. They have had experience using their senses to gather lists of descriptive words. Classes in the prewriting stage have pictorial lists, others have word lists. They have used Happy Talk so much, that with only a reminder at the beginning of the lesson, everyone will use it.

Lesson Overview
"Students, today your team members will meet in expert groups to brainstorm descriptive words that your team will use to write a story. These stories will be shared with the class. Everyone will be listening for descriptive words in the story. Of course, everyone will remember to use Happy Talk. Also, today we will check to see that everyone participates."

Lesson Overview
Jigsaw/Expert Groups:
Descriptive Words For Stories
A. Team Selection of Experts
The students meet in teams of four. Students number off and each team is given a packet of pictures containing pictures of dogs, children, plants, and buildings. "Students, when I say 'Number 1,' everyone with the #1 takes the picture of a dog. Everyone with the #2 takes the picture of a boy or girl. Everyone with the #3 takes the picture of a plant or tree. Everyone with the #4 takes the picture of a building."

B. Expert Groups: Preparation for Brainstorming

Students with the same type of pictures, take their pictures, and meet in the same corner of the room to form expert groups. Each expert group is given a large sheet of paper and a pencil or crayons for brainstorming their descrip-

---

Curran's Comments:

I find when I first do Jigsaw or with kindergarten or first grade students, I like to divide the large expert groups in each corner into sub groups. So if there were eight students in the dog expert group, I would divide that group into two smaller groups of four students each. Young students usually have a hard time working in a larger sized group. In large groups usually there are some who are so shy they don't want to participate or there are some who forget to use Happy Talk.

---

tive words/pictures. All the #1 students are in one corner with their dog pictures, all the #2 students are in another corner with their pictures of children, #3's with trees, and #4's with buildings.

C. Expert Groups: Gather Descriptive Words

Each expert group thinks of as many descriptive words as they can. The dog group would think of words such as; large, small, shaggy. Younger students draw pictures on the brainstorm sheet, older students write the words.

D. Roundrobin: Review the Brainstorm Ideas

"Expert groups, make sure each of your group members know what is on the brainstorm sheet by taking turns reading

the sheet to the group. Help each other remember what all the words/pictures are." Hang the brainstorm sheets for teams to refer to as they work on their stories.

Cooperative Project:

A. Teams Create Story

The experts go back to their teams. "Class in just a few minutes, each team is going to create a story that uses the objects from all four pictures in it. As each object is mentioned in the story, Person #1 is to ask the expert for that object to give some ideas of descriptive words that could be used for that object. Here are some ways you could ask the expert for descriptive words.

- What could we say about the dog?
- What words describe the dog?
- What did the expert group say about dogs?
- What words would tell about the dog?

The team will then decide on at least one of the descriptive words the expert suggests to use in the story. As the other objects are mentioned in the story, ask the child expert, the plant expert and the building expert for suggestions.

B. Illustrate Story and Evaluate Social Skill

Each team is given a large paper, crayons and scissors. They make an illustration to go with their story and glue the pictures onto the illustration. While they are working, check with person #1 on each team to see if everyone on the team contributed descriptive words to the story. Use the tally of their positive responses to praise or reward the teams for participation.

C. Practice the Story

The teams practice telling the story together several times until they feel they are ready to share the story with the whole class. Everyone participates in the presentation.

Team Inside-Outside Circle:

A. Share Stories

Half the teams are part of an inside circle. The other half pair up with an inner circle team as they form the outside circle. The inside teams tell their stories to the outside teams. Then the outside teams tell their stories. Finally, the outside teams rotate to a new inside circle team. Both teams tell their stories again.

B. Group Discussion: Evaluate Use of Descriptive Words

After each story is told, give the other teams a couple of minutes to discuss whether they heard all four objects mentioned in the story and descriptive words

---

Curran's Comments:

The students can work in their teams to gather pictures for this lesson. A day or two before you do this lesson, have the students do Lesson 14: Picture Hunt. Instead of looking for pictures of objects that start with a particular letter sound, they will be looking for pictures of dogs, children, trees and plants, and buildings.

---

for each. "Teams if you heard all four objects mentioned, raise one hand. If you heard descriptive words for each one, raise two hands." Call on a few students who have two hands up to tell you what descriptive words their team remembers hearing. Compliment or reward the

teams according to how many students have two hands raised.

Group Discussion/ Inside-Outside Circle:

Debrief the Lesson

Use Group Discussion in Team Inside-Outside Circle to find out how the students felt about the lesson by discussing some of the following questions. First give each team a minute to decide on an answer and choose a spokesperson. Then the teams share, rotate, and share on the next question with a new team.

* "How did it feel to work with an expert group to find out about words that would describe your object?"
* "How did it feel when the team asked you to suggest descriptive words?"
* "How did you feel about practicing the story with the group?"
* "How did you feel about telling the story to the class with your team?"

Variations:

* Objects can be changed to fit a theme, topic, or book the class is studying.
* The number of objects can vary to accommodate various sized groups: two objects for groups of two or six objects for groups of six.
* Older students can be given words instead of pictures.
* Teams can create another story by choosing different descriptive words in the story.
* Each team could be given a fifth object to put in their story. They would need to do their own brainstorming to find descriptive words for that object.

A Line for You: A Line for Me

Lesson 13

- ## Literature
Poem Stew
Read Aloud Rhymes
for the Very Young

- ## Grade Level
1-2

- ## Type of Lesson
Develop Oral Langauge: Creating
and Reciting Couplets

- ## Cognitive Objective
Students create a second line of a two line
poem using words from rhyming word families they have studied.

- ## Social Skills Objective
Polite Suggestions, Accepting Suggestions
Politely

- ## Materials
Colored team identification cards.

- *Class Discussion*
- *Group Discussion*
- *Numbered Heads*
- *Teams Share*
- *Stand and Share*

Structures

Background Information:

Students will have heard many stories and poems using rhyming words. The class has analyzed many of the rhymes to make oral and written lists of rhyming words. Some suggested titles are *Poem Stew* by Willam Cole and *Read Aloud Rhymes for the Very Young* by Jack Prelutsky.

Lesson Overview

"Today your teams can use the words from our Rhyming Word Family Charts to finish a poem that I start for you. While we make or receive suggestions as to how to finish the poem, we will use polite statements."

Lesson Sequence
Class Discussion
Ideas for Polite Suggestions

"Let's take a minute before we start our poems to think of some polite statements we could use as we make suggestions for the poem, or as we are responding to a team member who makes a suggestion." Record their ideas which may be similar to these:
"A word that would rhyme is _____ ."
"I think it would be funny to say _____."
"That's an idea we could use."
"That seems to be one of the best ideas."

Teams:
Create and Share Couplets, Model Couplets

Students meet in teams of three or four. "We are going to create two line poems called Couplets. To be a Couplet, the two lines must fit together. They must make sense together. Also the last words of each line must rhyme with each other. A sample would be:

I had a cow.
I wish I had it right now.

Group Discussion:
Create Couplets

"I will say the first line of the couplet and your team members will put their heads together to think of ideas that could be possible second lines. Use quiet six-inch voices. For example, I would say, 'I drove my car.' Then each team would start thinking of second lines like: 'Through the hot tar.' 'Not very far.' 'To get a candy bar.' You will have about five minutes to think of several ideas."

Teams Share:
Read Couplets

Give each team a different color team identification card. Then give the following directions so all teams pair up: "The yellow team and the green team meet together, the red team and the orange team meet together." Teams share with each other the possible endings their team has for the rhyme.

Group Discussion:
Create/Choose the Best Couplet

Students go back to their teams. "Each team will have about five minutes to think about all the rhyming lines you have heard. The team chooses the one they feel is the best, or possibly create a new line for the poem that is even better than the ones you have already heard. Make sure all the team members can say the line your team chooses."

Group Discussion/ Team Share:
Evaluate Giving and Accepting Suggestions

"Teams take a couple of minutes to remember any polite statements people on your team made while you were getting ideas and choosing the best second line for the rhyme. Choose one of the statements that the team would like to share with another team."

Stand and Share:
Positive Statements

Students on the teams number off. "Everyone please stand. I'll call a person number and a team color. The person with the number and team I call will share their team's positive statement. For example, if I say, 'Person #2 on green team,' Person #2 on the Green Team will tell the positive statement that the Green Team wanted to share and then the Green Team will sit down. If that was the same statement that any other team was going to share, that team sits down also." Record any new positive statements. Continue until all the teams are sitting down.

Numbered Heads Together:
Share the Rhymes

"In a moment, I am going to call a person's number to share the second line your team created. Take time now to make sure all the members of your team can say the second line." When practice time is over, say, "All #3 students please stand. When I call your team color you are to share the second line your team created as soon as I finish the first line."

Finger Signal Evaluation:

Recognition of Couplets

"If you feel the two lines did make a rhyme because they make sense together and the ending words of each line rhyme with each other, show thumbs up." A couple of students can be asked to validate their answer by telling how they know it is or is not a couplet. Continue the process until all the teams have had a chance to share. Continue to create more couplets.

Group Discussion:

Debrief the Lesson

Find out how the teams felt about working together in this lesson by having them discuss and share the following questions:

- What made it fun to make your team rhyme?
- How did using polite suggestions help your group work well together?
- What made it easy for your team to share the rhyme?
- Could anything have helped your team work even better?

Extensions:

- Team booklets are made as each team-member illustrates one of the couplets created in this lesson. They practice reading their booklet and do Team Share to read their booklet to other teams.
- Each team creates a beginning line that they tell the class so other teams can create couplets to go with that line.

Picture Hunt

Lesson 14

• Literature
Magazines & Newspapers

• Grade Level
K-1

• Cognitive Objective
Partners look in magazines and newspapers to find pictures of objects that start with a particular letter sound.

• Type of Lesson
Learning Letters: Identification of pictures or objects that start with certian sounds.

• Social Skills Objective
Take Turns

• Materials
Magazines or newspapers, scissors, envelopes, and pencils.

Structures
• **Cooperative Project**
• **Partners**
• **Think-Pair-Share**

Background Information
Students have had enough exposure to the letters and their sounds so they have a high degree of success recognizing a particular letter sound when they say the names of pictures or objects that start with that letter.

Lesson Overview
"Students, today you will work with a partner to find pictures of things in magazines or newspapers that start with a particular letter sound. Later in the lesson you will tell your team what pictures you found and you will see if they agree that the items in your pictures do start with the letter sound that has been assigned to you."

Lesson Sequence
Cooperative Project:
Pictures for Letter Sounds
A. Model Alternating Sounds
Call on a couple of students, each from a different team, to show how partners will alternate jobs. They decide who will be #1 and who will be #2. Give partner #1 a magazine and partner #2 a pair of scissors. The person with the magazine is responsible for turning pages, they both are responsible for looking at each page for pictures that contain objects that start with the letter sound that has been assigned to them. When they find a picture of an object that they agree starts with their letter sound, the partner with the scissors cuts that page out of the magazine (The objects will be cut out later in the lesson). Now they switch jobs. Partner #2 turns the pages and partner #1 has the scissors ready to cut out the next page they need.

Cooperative Project:
Pictures for Letter Sounds
A. Preparation for the Picture Hunt

Students go to their teams and form partners. In case of an odd number on the team, there may be some triads. The tasks in the triad would rotate also. The third person on the team can be the praiser who thinks of compliments to give their triad as they work. After the students have numbered off, give each team a magazine, a pair of scissors, and an envelope. Have the partners discuss who turns the page and who cuts. Check to see if they really understand what their job is by having them raise their hands when they hear you mention the job they are responsible for doing.

B. Assigning Letter Sounds

Assign letters so that within a team each set of partners is hunting for a different letter sound. Example: for a team of 4, one set of partners would be looking for pictures starting with the letter "a" sounds and the other set of partners would be looking for pictures that start with the "b" sound. Teams of 6 would be looking for "a", "b", and "c".

C. Partners: Do the Picture Hunt

Students hunt and cut until all of the partners have found several pages that have pictures of things that start with the letter sound assigned to them.

D. Cut out the Pictures

Instruct the partners to stop the picture hunt and to now work together to neatly cut out the pictures of the objects that start with their letter sound.

E. Clean Up

Partner #1 takes care of the paper scraps while partner #2 puts the pictures in the envelop.

F. Check and Study the Pictures

The partners check to see that all their pictures start with their letter sound. Also they make sure that both of them knows the names of all the pictures in their envelope.

Partners Discussion:
Alternating Jobs

If the partners agree that they did take turns with the jobs of turning pages and cutting out pages, they each put a happy face on their envelope.

Partners Share:
Show the Pictures

The partners now share the pictures in their envelope with their team. Partner #1 shows and tells about the first picture in their envelop, Partner #2 shows and tells about the second picture. They continue to alternate showing and telling until all the partners on the team have shared the pictures in their envelope. If the team is not sure whether a picture starts with that letter, the picture is set aside until all the pictures from their team have been shared. Then they check with the teacher.

Finger Signal Evaluation:

Sharing the Task

Count up the faces on the envelopes to praise or reward for sharing the tasks. Have the students give the thumbs up signal if the partners on their team took turns sharing the pictures from their envelopes.

Think-Pair-Share:

Debrief The Lesson

Find out how the partners felt about the lesson by having them Think, Pair, and then Share on the following questions.

- ✽ What did you and your partner learn about sharing jobs?
- ✽ What was the best thing about having a partner to help find and share pictures?

Variations:

- ✽ This lesson can be used for any combination of letters. This lesson can also be used for a word hunt, either words that start with a certain letter sound or words that fit a certain category.
- ✽ This lesson can be used to gather pictures that are needed for other lessons. Each team is responsible for gathering a particular type of picture that is needed for the lesson.

Extensions:

- ✽ Teams can use these pictures to make a collage of objects that start with a particular letter sound, see the Lesson 15: Alphabet Collage.
- ✽ Two teams can meet together to compile lists of all the different objects they found that start with that letter. These lists can be compiled to make a class list.

Alphabet Collage

Lesson 15

• Literature

Animal ABC
Animal Alphabet
Twenty Six Letters and 99 Cents
On Market Street
Alphabetics
Anno's Alphabet
Hambo Means Hello

• Grade Level

K-1

• Type of Lesson

Learning Letters: Recognition of beginning sounds

• Cognitive Objective

Students review letter sounds by categorizing pictures of objects that begin with certain sounds.

• Social Skills Objective

Pass Papers Politely

• Materials

An envelope of small pictures that begin with each of the letters used in the lesson, a set of collage papers, each one labeled with one of the letters used in the lesson.

- **Cooperative Project**
- **Group Discussion**
- **Simultaneous Roundtable**

Structures

Background Information

Students have heard alphabet stories that stress beginning sounds. They will have had experience making collections of items that begin with the letters used in today's lesson. Some suggested titles are: *Animal ABC* by Douglas Lee; *Animalia* by Graeme Base; *Animal Alphabet* by Bert Kitchen; *A,B,See* by Tana Hoban; *Twenty Six Letters and 99 Cents* by Tana Hoban; *On Market Street* by Arnold Lobel; *Alphabetics* by Suse MacDonald; *Anno's Alphabet* by Mitsumasa Anno; and *Hambo Means Hello* by Muriel Feeling.

Lesson Overview

"Students, today we are going to work together to make collages which show pictures of objects that start with the same letter. You will choose a picture, glue it on your paper and then politely pass your paper to the next person on your team when they are ready."

Lesson Sequence

Cooperative Project:

Categorize by Letter Sound

A. Preparation of Teams

Each team of four is given an envelope that contains a few pictures of items that start with each of these letters: A, B, C, and D. The pictures are taken out of the envelope and laid in the middle of the table. Each team is given a set of papers that have been labeled from A to D. The team members number off from one to four. Person #1 takes the paper labeled A, person #2 takes B, person #3 takes C, and person #4 takes D.

B. Simultaneous Roundtable: Hunt and Glue

When the teacher says to begin, each team member finds a picture that starts with the same as the letter that is written at the top of their paper. (Person #1 finds a picture that starts with an "A" sound and glues it to their paper, and passes the paper when Person #2 is ready. Person #2 finds a picture that starts with the "B" sound and glues it to their paper, and passes the paper when Person #3 is ready.) The students continue looking for pictures, gluing pictures, and passing papers.

C. Finger Evaluation: Use of Polite Passing

After each team has passed papers several times, show the silent signal. Ask the students to show thumbs up if the person who passes the papers is waiting until they are ready before the paper is passed. Remind the students to be polite passers as they continue.

Group Discussion:
Stop and Edit

After each team has several pictures on each of the letter sheets, signal that it is time to stop. Person #1 puts the extra pictures in the envelope. Person #2 puts away the glue bottles. Then the team checks to see that the correct pictures are on each letter sheet.

Group Discussion:
Evaluate Polite Passing

Each team member decides if they feel that the letter papers were passed to them only when they were ready. If they feel they were, they write a happy face in a bottom corner of the paper. Count up the happy faces in each team to give them praise or rewards.

Group Discussion:
Debrief the Lesson

Find out how the teams felt about the lesson by having them discuss and share the following questions:

* What did your team do that helped the papers pass quickly and easily?
* What could the team do to make this job even easier?
* "What did the team do that helped you do your best job?"
* "What did the team do that helped them get the collages done?"

Variations:

* The lesson can be used with any combination of letters.
* The lesson could compliment a story such as *Crictor* by Tomi Ungerer in which the students would make collages for the letters that Crictor could shape with his body.
* Use pictures of letter blends for first and second graders.
* Use the lesson format to categorize animals, birds, fish, reptiles.
* Use the lesson format to categorize food groups.

Curran's Comments:

Use Lesson 14, Picture Hunt to have the students gather the pictures necessary for this lesson. Pictures gathered by one team could be used by another team to make their collage. Or if two classes do both lessons, the classes could swap pictures and share collages with each other.

Help Me With ABC

Lesson 16

• Literature

Animal ABC
Animal Alphabet
Twenty Six Letters and 99 Cents
On Market Street
Alphabetics
Anno's Alphabet
Hambo Means Hello

• Grade Level

K-2

• Type of Lesson

Learning Letters: Recognition
of letter names

• Cognitive Objective

Pairs of students help each other remember
the names of alphabet letters.

• Social Skills Objective

Active Listening, Happy Talk

• Materials

Color-Coded Co-op Cards, four sets of alphabet cards per team, each in a different color, paper and
crayons to practice writing letters.

Structures

- **Color-Coded Co-op Cards**
- **Partners**
- **Group/Class Discussion**

Background Information

The class has heard many alphabet stories such as those listed in Lesson 15: Alphabet Collage. They have discussed and practiced the names of the letters until they know most of them quite well.

Lesson Overview

"Each of you will be with a partner who will check to see how many of the alphabet cards you already know. Then you will help each other practice the letters you still need to learn. While you work, you both need to be active listeners so you can help each other learn the letters."

Lesson Sequence

Color-Coded Co-op Cards:

Names of Alphabet Letters

A. Preparation for Co-op Cards

Students meet in teams of four and number off from one to four. Numbers one and two become partners and numbers three and four become partners. Each student is given a set of Color-Coded Co-op Cards. There is a different color for each member of the team.

B. Model Use of Cards /Ideas for Happy Talk

Call two students to model the use of Color-Coded Co-op Cards as you explain it. "Students, when it is time to start, you

---

will give each other a pretest to see how many of the letters you already know. Person #1 will give their cards to Person #2. Person #2 will show person #1 their letter cards one at a time. If the letter name is said correctly, Person #2 gives the card back to person #1 and gives Person #1 Happy Talk, like 'Great Memory,' or 'Fantastic Job.' If Person #1 did not say the card correctly, Person #2 will keep the card so it can be studied later. After Person #1 has finished saying all the cards, Person #2 gives their cards to Person #1. Person #2 will now show Person #2 the cards, giving the ones that are said correctly back to Person #2 and keeping the rest of the cards for studying. Now both partners put the cards they said correctly in back of them. At this time you need to teach your partner the letters they still need to know. Person #2 shows Person #1 each of his/her cards and teaches them the letter name. Then Person #1 does the same for Person #2. You keep on practicing until both of you know all the letter names. Remember to keep using Happy talk statements."

Partners:

Practice the Co-op Cards

"Now you are ready to do the Color-Coded Co-op Cards. If you both get stuck on a letter, quietly ask the other partners on your team to help you. If none of you know what the letter is, you have a team question so all of you raise your hands and I will come to help you. If you finish before the others are done, you may use the paper to practice writing the letters." Monitor how well the students are doing. When all the partners have finished, or a reasonable length of study time has passed, evaluate Active Listening.

Finger Evaluation:

Use of Happy Talk

"Students, if you feel your partner used Active Listening while you were working together give a thumbs up signal. Tell your partner what Happy Talk they used. Repeat some of the happy talk you heard.

Curran's Comments:

Sometimes I collect the cards that were in front of students to keep in an envelop marked with the group number. By checking the frequency with which the letters were missed within the teams, I know which letters to emphasize in our class activities. Then the next day I return the cards to the teams so they can continue the Color Coded Co-op Card study.

Partners Share with Team:

Cards and Written Letters

Students meet back in their teams of four. They take turns saying their Color Coded Co-op Cards by starting with Person #1 and ending with Person #4. "As you say your cards, put a happy face on the ones you say correctly and put them in the center of the table. Put any cards you still had difficulty remembering in a pile in front of you." When everyone has finished saying their cards, they may read to the team any letters they had time to write. When you notice a team is done saying their cards, have them tell you how well they did. Have Person #4 count the cards in the center. Record the number. Total the numbers to find out how many cards the whole class got correct. Praise them for how many they got correct. Return the cards to their owners.

Partners/Teams:

Repeat Co-op Cards Practice

Repeat the practice, using just the cards without happy faces — those they still need to learn. When the practice is repeated, the teams are trying to improve their own score by having more cards in the center pile. Check with each team as they finish saying their cards. Praise or reward the class for the number of teams that improved their score.

Group/Class Discussion:

Debrief the Lesson

Find out how the teams felt about the lesson by having the teams discuss the following questions:

- What was the best thing about practicing the letter cards with your partner?
- What made this activity fun?
- What could have been better?

Other Applications:

- Students help each other learn the letter sounds.
- Students help each other learn vocabulary words from a story.

Quick Write Right

• Literature

Animal ABC
Animal Alphabet
Twenty Six Letters and 99 Cents
On Market Street
Alphabetics
Anno's Alphabet
Hambo Means Hello

• Grade Level

K-1

• Type of Lesson

Learning Letters: Recall of
Letters and Writing

• Cognitive Objective

Practice remembering and writing
letters of the alphabet.

• Social Skills Objective

Quick work, Taking Turns

• Materials

A Roundtable Sequence board for each group (see Lesson 11: Recite A Rhyme),
a folded piece of lined paper and pencil for each group.

Structures

• *Group Discussion*
• *Roundrobin*
• *Sequential Roundtable*
• *Teams Share*

Lesson Overview

"Today we are going to learn a fun way to remember the letters of the alphabet and practice writing the letters. We are going to do a Roundtable writing game where all the team members work together to write as many of the letters of the alphabet as they can in about five minutes."

Lesson Sequence
Sequential Roundtable:

Review of Letter Writing
A. Demonstrate Use of Roundtable Sequence Board
Choose three students to work with you as a demonstration team. Sit around the Roundtable Sequence Board. (See Lesson

11: Recite A Rhyme) Person #1 has a folded piece of lined paper and a pencil. Person #1 writes any letter of the alphabet and follows the arrows on the game board to pass the paper to Person #2 who writes a different letter and passes it to the next person. Continue for a couple more passes, then stop.

B. Class Discussion: Analyze Roundtable
Ask the class what things the demonstration team did that made the Roundtable game easy. You could hear responses such as these. "They waited quietly." "They waited for their turns." "They were ready for their turn." Praise the students for their great ideas. Point out that their objectives today are to work quietly and take turns so their team will have a chance to write many letters during the game.

C. Preparation Of Teams

Students meet in teams of four. Each team is given a Roundtable Sequence Board. Person #1 is given a lined piece of paper that has been folded in half and a pencil. When the teacher says to start, they will keep the paper folded in half and take turns writing and passing until the teacher gives the signal to stop. Remind them, "Each time you must write a letter that is not on your team's paper yet. If one of your team members can not think of a letter, the team members may whisper a suggestion. Remember to work quickly and take turns. I will stop you after a couple of minutes to see how you are doing. You may start."

Sequential Roundtable:

Teams Write Letters

The teams write and pass for three or four minutes. Check to see that everyone is using the arrows on the sequence board to help them pass the paper the right direction. Also point out which groups are being very successful writing and passing the paper.

Group Discussion:

Ideas for Taking Turns / Working Quickly

Ask the teams to stop and show Active Listening. Have them talk over answers to these questions.
• "Are you working quickly?"
• "Are you taking turns?"
• "How are you doing these things?"
Have some of the groups share their answers. Now ask whichever team member has the paper in front of them to count up how many letters their team has.

Share the results this way:

"Teams that have at least six letters stand up." (Be sure the number is lower than the lowest number any group has so all will get to stand up.) "At least ten letters stay standing, others sit down. At least fifteen." Ask the top scoring groups to share what they did to help them do so well. Responses could be: "We watch so we are ready to take the paper and pencil." "We are thinking of some letters that are left so we are ready to write." Give the teams a couple of minutes to think about the suggestions they have heard to see how their group can work even better.

Sequential Roundtable:

Continue Writing Letters

Have the teams open up their lined papers and continue writing the alphabet, but write the new letters on the other half of the paper so they can see if they go any faster now that they have thought of some suggestions to help their team. The teams continue to write for another three or four minutes.

Group Discussion:

Improvement in Taking Turns and Working Quickly

Again have the teams count the letters on the second half of the paper and see if they have more than on the first half of the paper. Give the teams a minute to think why their team did better, the same, or maybe worse. Have them choose someone who will share the response with the class. Then have the class give a quick response to these questions by raising their hands.

- How many feel your team worked quickly today?
- How many feel your team got quicker as you played the game?
- How many feel your team helped each other by taking turns?

Comment on the number of hands as validation that the teams did well on the behavioral objectives today.

Roundrobin:

Teams Practice Reading Letters
The teams practice reading the letters they wrote using Roundrobin.

Teams Share:

Read Letters in Another Team
Then two teams get to share their letters. Have one team Roundrobin to read the letters while the other team listens. When the first team finishes, the second team begins.

Group Discussion:

Debrief the Lesson
Debrief the lesson by discussing the following questions to find out how the teams felt about working together.

What did your team do to:
- Help pass papers quickly?
- Help team members when it was their turn?
- Help your team members enjoy the lesson?

Variations:

- Number writing review
- Spelling word review
- During the Roundtable, letters must be written in alphabetical order

Extensions:

- Teams can agree on a pattern made of alphabet letters. As the paper is passed on the sequence board they add the next letter in the pattern.
- The teams make illustrations to go with each letter on their sequence sheet that shows objects that start with that letter. Older students make lists of words that start with the letters on their sheet.
- Teams use the Alphabet Chart to find which letters they left out. They each write some of the left out letters on slips of paper which are glued to make a group a letter collage.

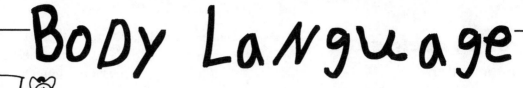

Body Language

Lesson 18

• Literature
Alphabetics
ABC Alphabet Rhymes

• Grade Level
K-1

• Type of Lesson
Learning Letters:
Forming Letters

• Cognitive Objective
Teams of students use their bodies to
shape letters of the alphabet.

• Social Skills Objective
Everyone Participates, Polite Suggestions

• Materials
A paper and pencil for each group.

- **Class Discussion**
- **Formations**
- **Group Discussion**
- **Teams**
- **Think-Pair-Share**

Structures

Background Information
The students are quite familiar with the names and shapes of the letters. Some suggested titles for literature are: *Alphabetics* by Suse MacDonald, *ABC Alphabet Rhymes* by Edward Leer.

Lesson Overview
"We have been studying the letters of the alphabet. Today our teams will decide how to use our bodies to shape the letters of the alphabet. We want to be sure everyone on the team is part of each letter formation. When it is our turn to help the team shape the letter correctly, we need to remember how to give suggestions in a polite way."

Lesson Sequence
Class Discussion:
Ideas for Giving Suggestions
"One job you will do is give suggestions for fixing the shape of the team letter, so let us think of some of the things you can say." Write down their suggestions. Some of their suggestions may be like the following. "It would help if you would move this way a little bit." "Could you move your arm over here please." "Please lean in. That will help."

Formations:
Review Letter Shapes
A. Preparation of Groups
The students meet in teams of three or four and number off. Each team is given a paper and pencil.

Group Discussion:

Plan the Letter

"I will tell you a letter. Person #1 writes the letter on the paper. See if you agree that is the correct shape for the letter or if it needs to be changed. When it looks just right, decide how all of you will work together to make the letter shape with your bodies."

Teams:

Form and Check the Letter

"Each person is to stand in their place. Person #2 checks to see if the team's letter is the right shape and gives suggestions for changing positions or compliments for a job well done." Check the letter shapes and give any final suggestions for shaping the letter and compliments and or points for completing the letter.

Finger Evaluation:

Positive Suggestions

"All teams who heard Person #2 use positive suggestions or compliments give the thumbs up signal." Praise or reward according to how many signals you see. Add any new positive statements to the class list.

Teams:

Rotate Jobs

Make more letters. Rotate jobs so that Person #2 writes the letter and Person #3

checks the letter. For the third letter the team makes, Person #3 writes the letter, while Person #4 checks the letter formation.

Think-Pair-Share:

Debrief the Lesson

Find out how the students felt about the lesson by having the students form partners within the team so they can think to themselves, discuss with their partner, and share with their team. Listen as the teams share, and share with the class some of the comments you heard. Ask the the following questions:

- What did your team do that make it easy to form the letters?
- Was it easy or hard to write the letter for your team? Why?
- What did the team learn about giving and taking suggestions?

Variations:

- For very young students, the teacher can provide the shapes on the blackboard or chart rack.
- Students can form numbers, words, and number sentences.
- Students can join as a class to form one large letter, number, happy face, or ice cream cone.
- Students can create a machine or an appliance from a story and include the motion and sound.

Leaf Line-Up

Lesson 19

• Literature

The Alphabet Tree

• Grade Level
K-1

• Type of Lesson
Learning Letters: Alphabetical Order

• Cognitive Objective
Students will recall alphabetical order by finding the correct placement for their letter in the alphabet.

• Social Skills Objective
Polite Suggestions

• Materials
An alphabet leaf for each student (blank leaves are included), yarn for the line-up, label cards beginning, middle, end, and tape.

- Line-Ups
- Partner Discussion
- Think-Pair-Share

Structures

Background Information

A good motivation for this lesson will be the story *The Alphabet Tree* by Leo Lionni. The students are able to recognize the letters of the alphabet and can say the letters in alphabetical order. They have had some practice putting letters in alphabetical order.

Lesson Overview

"We are going make a Line-Up so that the leaves we are given, with the letters of the alphabet on them, will be in alphabetical order. If you need to suggest that someone else needs to change positions, you need to give these suggestions in a polite way."

Lesson Sequence:

Line-Ups:

Review Alphabetical Order

A. Class Discussion: Ideas for Polite Suggestions

"Students, let's think of some polite ways you could suggest that you or someone else needs to move or stay in the same place." As they offer suggestions similar to these, write them on a chart (They will also be used in Lesson 20). "I think I need to move over here." "You probably should be on this side." "Could you please move over here?" "Great, I think we are just right."

B. Preparation for the Line-Up

Lay a long piece of yarn across the room; with one end labeled "A", the center labeled "M", and the other end labeled

---

...student is given a leaf with a ...letter of the alphabet written on

C. Do the Line-Up

"Everyone think where your letter goes; at the beginning, in the middle, or at the end of the alphabet. In a few minutes, you will take your leaf and stand in that part of the Line-Up where you think your letter would go. You will quietly talk to the students around you and politely give suggestions as to where you and others should stand so the Line-Up will be in alphabetical order."

Curran's Comments:

If the students haven't done Line-Ups very much, you might find it helpful to model the Line-Up with several children, using leaves with numbers on them. Once the class sees the students do the numbers Line-Up, they will understand how to do the alphabet Line-Up.

Finger Evaluation:

Recognition of Alphabetical Order

When everyone is standing in the Line-Up, give these directions. "Starting at the beginning of the Line-Up, everyone in order will say the letter that is on their leaf. Listen to see if it sounds like the leaves are in alphabetical order." All the students say their letters. The students vote thumbs up if they feel the letters are in alphabetical order, or thumbs down if they feel the letters are not in alphabetical order. Look at the signals. Have

them work to correct the Line-Up if some of the letters are still out of order. Praise or reward the students when they have the Line-Up in the correct order.

Keep Line-Up Information

When the leaves in the Line-Up are in the correct order, give the students a piece of tape. They can tape their leaf to the yarn so the results of the Line-Up can be kept.

Partner Discussion:

Use of Polite Statements

The students number off one, two, three, four, along the line. The one's face the two's and the three's face the four's. They discuss with each other any polite statements they heard. As they are discussing with each other, move along the line and listen to the polite statements they are sharing. Have the students give the silent signal and then signal thumbs up if they heard polite statements and thumbs down if they didn't hear polite statements. Call on a few of the students to give reasons for their signal. You can share a couple of the polite statements you heard also. Add any new statements to the class list.

Curran's Comments:

Sometimes I find it helpful to record their answers so I can play back what they say if they give a split vote or if many of the students are not sure what the answer should be. All I do in this case, is play the tape of the students saying their letters, and point to the alphabet at the same time. This way the students have an easier time checking to see if their letter order was correct.

Think-Pair-Share:

Debrief the Lesson

To find out how the students felt about the lesson, have them discuss some of the following questions with the same partner:

- How did you feel about taking your leaf to the Line-Up?
- What made it easy for you to find the place for your letter in the line up?
- Was it easy or hard to use polite statements as you gave suggestions? What made it easy or hard?
- Think about polite statements you heard today? Say that polite statement to your partner so you can remember it to use another time.

Variations:

- Use the numbers one to thirty and have the students find out where his/her numbers would be placed in the Line-Up.
- An easier version of the Line-Up for the younger students would be to have the letters labeled along the Line-Up and they match the letter on their leaf to the letter on the Line-Up.
- Use adding machine tape for the labeled line. The students can then glue their leaf to the tape after they finish the Line-Up.
- Another easy version is that the capital letters are along the Line-Up, and the students have cards with lower-case letters that they must match to the upper-case letters on the Line-Up.

Extensions:

- The class makes a tree alphabet book by thinking of a word that tells something about trees for each letter of the alphabet. Each student draws the page showing the letter he put on the alphabet Line-Up.

Example:

- A for apple tree
- B for bark
- C for cut down
- D for dirt
- E for evergreen tree

The Alphabet Tree

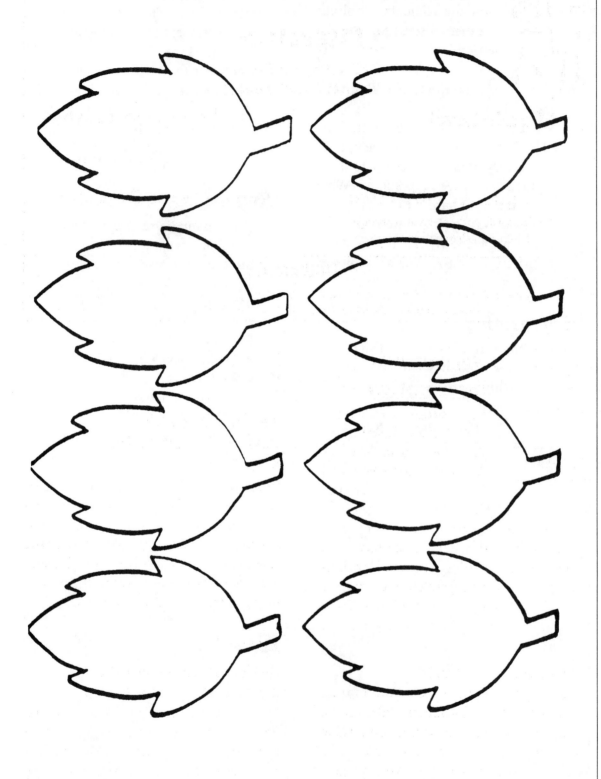

Lorna Curran: *Lessons for Little Ones: Language Arts*©
Kagan Cooperative Learning • 1 (800) Wee Co-op

Foliage For a Few

Lesson 20

• Literature
The Alphabet Tree
Brian Wildsmith's ABC

• Grade Level
K-2

• Type of Lesson
Learning Letters:
Alphabetizing Letters

• Cognitive Objective
Students will work together to arrange letters into alphabetical order.

• Social Skills Objective
Polite Suggestions

• Materials
A piece of yarn about 8 feet long for each team, a set of leaves for each team with alphabet written on them (use leaves from Lesson 19: Leaf Line-Up), and tape.

Structures
• *Choral Response*
• *Class Discussion*
• *Group Discussion*
• *Line-Ups*

Background Information

The students will have looked at and heard many alphabet stories such as the ones listed below and in Lesson 15: Alphabet Collage. They are able to recognize the letters of the alphabet and say the letters in alphabetical order. They have had some practice putting letters in alphabetical order. Some suggested titles are: *The Alphabet Tree* by Leo Lionni and *Brian Wildsmith's ABC* by Brian Wildsmith.

Lesson Overview

"Your teams will have the task of putting the letters of the alphabet in order on the line up yarn. Each of you is responsible for putting your letters on the line. You will help each other by making suggestions as to where the letters should be placed so that all of them are in the correct order."

Lesson Sequence
Review Ideas for Polite Suggestions

Read over the Polite Suggestions Chart the students made in Lesson 19: Leaf Line-Up. "Remember to use these suggestions and remember any new polite suggestions you make when you give suggestions to each other. We will add these to the chart at the end of the lesson."

Line-Ups:
Review of Alphabetical Order
A. Preparation for the Line-Up
Students meet in teams of four to six. Each team is given a piece of yarn about eight feet long. In each team, the person with the first name that starts with the letter closest to the beginning of the

alphabet, lays the yarn out in a straight line near the team. Each team gets a packet of leaves with the letters of the alphabet written on them. The team passes out the leaves so each team member has an equal number. The team is given a box of crayons. Each team member takes a different color crayon and draws a circle around the edge of the leaves that have been passed to him/her. This color codes the leaves so we can see that each team member places an equal number of leaves on the Line-Up.

B. Group Discussion: Do the Line-Up
Lay "Start" and "End" labels on each team's piece of yarn. The teammembers work together to lay out the leaves in alphabetical order. "Teams, work together to lay out your leaves so they are in alphabetical order. The person who has the letter 'A,' will lay it by the word 'Start.' The person who has the letter 'B,' will lay it down next to the letter 'A.' Continue doing this until everyone has laid out all their letters. Read the letters to see if you agree they are in alphabetical order. When you do agree, use tape to fasten the leaves to the yarn. Remember when you give suggestions to use polite statements like we mentioned earlier in the lesson."

Group Discussion:
Evaluate Giving Polite Suggestions
The teams are given a minute to remember what polite statements they used as they gave suggestions. Call on one person from each team to share with the class a polite statement their team used. Record new statements on the chart.

Choral Response:
Recognition of Alphabetical Order
As the team Line-Ups are hung, the class says the letters in alphabetical order to check and see if the Line-Up is correct. Praise or reward each of the teams who have arranged all the leaves in perfect alphabetical order.

Group/Class Discussion:
Debrief the Lesson
Find out how the teams felt about the lesson by having them discuss the following questions:
- What did your team learn today about working together?
- What made it easy or hard to give polite suggestions?
- How did you feel when your team's line up was shared? Why?

Variations:
- If you use a book with another theme, like the *Icky Bug Book* by Jerry Palotta make the letters on shapes that match the theme of the book. In this case the students would get bug shapes. Each team might like to design their own bug shape that you could ditto for them.
- On the back side of each leaf, they could draw an object that starts with that letter.
- Each team gets blank leaves. Team members number off. Assign the letters in scrambled fashion so that each team member writes letters on an

equal number of leaves. They use these leaves to make their alphabetical order.

Extensions:

* Use this procedure to have students alphabetize groups of words.
* Teams can arrange days of the week or months of the year in the correct sequence.
* To build in individual accountability for older students, they would individually write the letters in alphabetical order.

Who Did It?

Lesson 21

• Literature

The Three Little Pigs

• Grade Level
K-2

• Type of Lesson
Ready Skills: Recall Story Events

• Cognitive Objective
Students think together to recall the actions of characters in a story.

• Social Skills Objective
Quiet Voices

• Materials
Character cards - one set per team.

• Group Discussion

• Numbered Heads

Structures

Background Information

Students have heard a story many times so they are familiar with what the characters do in the story. This lesson is done after the students have heard the story *The Three Little Pigs* by Paul Galdone. The students have used quiet voices as they have done other lessons so they only need a reminder to use them in this lesson.

Lesson Overview

"We have heard the story The Three Little Pigs several times. When you get in teams today, I am going to ask you a question about something that happened in the story. You will need to talk it over and decide which character did or said the thing I am asking you about. You

will then find that character's name on your team's answer cards and have it ready to show to the class."

Lesson Sequence

Numbered Heads:

Remember Story Events

A. Preparation for Numbered Heads

Students meet in teams of four. Each team is given a set of character cards with the names of a story characters on them. Team members number off from one to four.

B. Numbered Heads Together: Decide on Team Answer

"Listen to my question. Discuss the answer until everyone agrees on an answer. Find the character card that shows the right answer. Remember to use quiet voices so the other groups don't

---

hear you discussing the answers. 'What character in the story built a house of twigs? Talk it over."

C. Appropriate Team Member Show Answer
"Person #2 on each team share your answer by holding the correct character card above your head. Good, I see that all teams are holding up the correct card that says, 'second pig.' Teams you did a good job of talking over the answer."

D. Team Points for Correct Answers
Each time the answers are shared, give points for the teams that have the correct answer. Tally the points at the end to see if the class could recall the characters who did certain actions in the story.

Repeat Numbered Heads Together
Continue asking questions about The Three Little Pigs such as:
- What character built a house of sticks?
- What character liked to trick people?
- Which character put a pot of water on to boil?
- What character was the safest in his house?

Each time choose a different person number for sharing the answers.

Group Discussion/ Finger Evaluation:
Use of Quiet Voices
Give the teams a minute to review how they did in using Quiet Voices. "Signal how well the team did when I say 'One, Two, Three, Show.' Signal five fingers to

show, 'Yes we used quiet voices.' Signal three fingers to show, 'We used quiet voices most of the time.' Signal one finger to show, 'Oops we used quiet voices just some of the time."

Numbered Heads Together:
Debrief the Lesson
Find out how the teams felt about doing the lesson together by discussing some of the following questions.

What things did your team do that made it easy to:
- "Find out which character was the right answer?"
- "Show the answer card for your team?"
- "To use a quiet voice while the team made its decisions?"

Variations:
- All the students can have character cards and show them at the same time when it is time to answer. Numbered Heads Together can still be used to select someone to give the answer but everyone would have their own cards to manipulate.
- Response cards can be used with any story that has several characters, events, and/or places.
- The answer cards could be titles of books. Events from the different stories would be told and the team would have to decide in which story the events happened.

Student Response Cards

1ˢᵀ PIG

2ᴺᴰ PIG

3ᴿᴰ PIG

WOLF

Lorna Curran: *Lessons for Little Ones: Language Arts*©
Kagan Cooperative Learning • 1 (800) Wee Co-op   **Lesson 21: 3**

Cat Catastrophes

• Literature

Millions of Cats

• Grade Level

K-2

• Type of Lesson

Reading Skills: Prediction

• Cognitive Objective

Students predict problems that could occur from having a large number of cats.

• Social Skills Objective

Paraphrasing

• Materials

Ditto of cat shapes if you want to do the background activity of making a 100 cat mural or a kitten graph from the extensions.

Structures

• Think-Pair-Share
• Class Discussion

Background Information

The students have heard the story *Millions Of Cats* by Wanda Gag. The students have read this sentence from the story, "Hundreds of cats, thousands of cats, millions, and billions and trillions of cats." The students will know how many a hundred cats are by putting together a mural showing 100 cats or by putting together 100 unifix cubes. They have tried to imagine how many a hundred of those hundreds would be for a thousand, and then have imagined a million, billion and trillion.

Lesson Overview

"We heard the story Millions of Cats. We saw how many 100 is and have tried to imagine a thousand, million, billion, and trillion. Now we are going to talk with a partner about what it could be like to have so many cats. As we discuss our ideas with our partners, we will paraphrase or say back to them what they told us. This will let them know that we heard and understand what they said."

Lesson Sequence

Class Discussion:

Examples of Paraphrasing

"When we paraphrase, we use our own words to tell our partners what we think they said. For example, if the teacher asked, 'How many is a billion cats?' and my partner said 'I think a billion cats would be an awful lot of cats.' I could say that idea back to my partner by saying, 'You think a billion cats would be a huge bunch of cats.' or 'Your idea is a billion would be too many cats.' If this is the first time the class has done paraphrasing, you might like to give them a couple more sentences to share with the class possible ways to paraphrase. Record the underlined gambits to make a Paraphrase Chart.

Think-Pair-Share:
Predict Problems
A. Assign Partners
Let the students know who their partners are. Either give them cards numbered 1 or 2, or have them decide who will be person #1 to share first and who will be person #2 who will share second.

B. Think of an Answer
"I am going to ask you a question about those billions of cats. Then I am going to give you a minute to think of some answers inside your head."

Some questions that could be asked are:
* Which cat do you think the very old man should have taken home and why?
* How did the wife feel when she saw the cats the very old man brought home?
* Why did she say they couldn't keep the cats?
* What problems would they have had if they kept all the billions of cats?

C. Pairs Share Ideas and Paraphrase
"Now you will tell your ideas to each other. Person #1 tell your ideas to your partner, then your partner will paraphrase what you said to let you know he understood. Then person #2 tells their ideas and their partner paraphrases what was said. If your partner didn't understand what you said, you may need to tell them again in a different way. Then your partner would again paraphrase what you said."

D. Share Ideas with the Class
Ask for the silent signal. "Now anyone that would like to share an idea about the old man and his cats that you said or heard, raise your hands so we can share some of our answers."

Hand Signal:
Check for Paraphrasing
"Those of you who paraphrased what your partner said, raise one hand. Those of you who also heard your partner paraphrase what you said, raise your other hand." Look for inconsistencies where one partner has 2 hands up and the other only has 1 hand up. It could be that a person thought they paraphrased, but they really didn't; or it could be a person paraphrased, but the partner didn't recognize it as paraphrasing. To validate the good job they did, let them know what you saw and heard while you observed them. Ask the students if their are any new gambits to add to the Paraphrasing Chart.

Think-Pair-Share:
Debrief the Lesson
Find out how the students felt about working together in Think-Pair-Share by discussing the following questions.
* How did it help you to have a couple of minutes to think of answers before you talked to anyone?
* What did your partner do that made it easy to share answers and paraphrase?
* How did the paraphrasing beforehand make it easier to share with the class?

Variations:
* Use without the paraphrasing for a faster process.

- Instead of paraphrasing have them repeat the statement exactly as it was said. This method is easier for the kindergarten students.

Other Applications:

- Used in a class discussion so they can practice an answer before they say it for the class.
- Used to get everyone involved in a discussion quickly. For example "Guess what you think will happen next."
- Used for everyone to express a prediction to some one before finding out the solution.

Extensions:

- Use Think-Pair-Share to discuss, "If you were going to a pet shop or to the home of a mother cat who had kittens to choose a cat for yourself or a friend, how would you decide which cat to pick?"
- If they were to choose a kitten for themselves or a friend, what color would they choose? Use the kitten pictures that are included to make a graph.
- How many cats would be too many cats for you?
- If you had too many cats, what could you do?

Cat Pictures

Brainstorming Blue

or draw ... be the ... to

• Literature

*Beside The Bay
Mary Wore Her Red Dress
Hailstones & Halibut Bones
A Color Of His Own
Little Blue, Little Yellow
Brown Bear, Brown Bear,
What Do You See?*

• Grade Level

K-2

• Type of Lesson

Reading Skills: Develop Color
Word Banks

• Cognitive Objective

Students brainstorm many words or
pictures of objects that belong to a
particular color category.

• Social Skills Objective

Quiet Voices, Quick Work

• Materials

Brainstorm sheets: 1 of each of 4 different colors per group, pencils and crayons.

Structures

- **Roundrobin**
- **Simultaneous Roundtable**
- **Team Share**

Background Information

Students know the names of the colors and can identify objects of a specific color. They have heard many stories about color such as: *Beside The Bay* by Sheila Samton; *Mary Wore Her Red Dress* by Merle Peek; *Hailstones and Halibut Bones* by Mary O'Neill; *A Color Of His Own* by Leo Lionni; *Little Blue, Little Yellow* by Leo Lionni; *Brown Bear, Brown Bear, What Do You See* by Bill Martin.

Lesson Overview

As each student receives a paper with a particular color written on it, they add a word or picture that represents an object that would be that color. They then pass that paper and receive another with a different color word on it. Again they add a word or picture and pass the paper. After

there are several words on each sheet, the team members practice reading the items on their brainstorm sheet so they can be shared with other groups.

Lesson Sequence
Simultaneous Roundtable:

Strengthening Color Concepts

A. Preparation for Roundtable

Students meet in teams of four. Each team receives four brainstorm sheets with a different color word printed on each one. Each team member takes one of the brainstorm sheets and a pencil. Take a minute and have them practice passing their papers and pencils to the right around the group.

B. Simultaneous Brainstorming: Add Ideas to Brainstorm Sheets

The team members look at the color word at the top of their brainstorm sheets and write the word for an object

---

a picture of an object that would
at color. Then they pass the paper
the right and quietly wait for the paper
om the person on their left. Everyone
now has a sheet with a new color word.
They add a word or picture for an object
of that color and pass again. The team
keeps on passing papers for about 10
minutes.

Recognition of Working Quickly and Quietly

Each person looks at the bottom corners
of their brainstorm sheet. If they feel
their teammates worked quickly, they circle the runner. If they feel their group
worked quietly, they circle the person
giving the quiet signal. Ask a few of the
students why they had circled either or
both of the answers. Then count the
number of students who had circled the
runner to give praise or reward for working quickly. Count up the quiet signals
circled to praise or reward for working
quietly.

Practice Reading the Brainstorm Sheets

Each person on the team reads the brainstorm sheet that is in front of him/her as
the team helps clarify what the
words/pictures are.

Team Share:

Read the Brainstorm Sheets

Assign teams who will meet together to
share their brainstorm sheets with each
other. The eight students number off
around the circle. Person #1 shares
his/her brainstorm first, then Person #2,
Person #3, etc. Collect and save the
brainstorm sheets to use as a resource for
writing activities.

Roundrobin:
Debrief the Lesson

Find out how the teams felt about the
lesson by using Roundrobin to discuss
the following questions:
What did your group do that made it
easy to:
* Add words to the brainstorm sheet?
* Pass the paper quickly and quietly?
* Learn all the words on the brainstorm sheet?

Variations:

* Kindergarten and beginning first
  grade students who are still unfamiliar
  with all the color words, could take
  time to color in the frame around
  their color word so everyone will
  remember what color items go on that
  brainstorm sheet.
* Students having the same color can be
  grouped together. They number off.
  Person #1 reads their list and Person
  #2 adds any new words. Then Person
  #3 adds any new words and so on,
  until they have a composite list.

Extensions:

Use the color brainstorm to:
* Make color picture books where each
  team member makes a neat illustration for one of the objects from each
  of the color sheets. Then they make a
  sentence for each illustration. If each
  team member chooses a different
  object from each color sheet, a group
  of four produce a booklet containing
  four colors.
* Make color chants (see Lesson 30)
* Make color poetry (see Lesson 32)

Color Words

Yellow

Orange

Red

Green

Color Words

Blue

Purple

Brown

Black

Color Words

Red

Definition Dilemma

Lesson 24

• Grade Level
K-2

• Literature
Where the Wild Things Are

• Type of Lesson
Reading Skills: Using story context to define unfamiliar word

• Cognitive Objective
Students decide upon the definition of a rumpus using contextual clues & make a mural that matches description.

• Social Skills Objective
Polite Suggestions, Accepting Suggestions Politely

• Materials
Team number cards - stand up cards with a number for each team, large paper to list Polite Suggestions.

Structures
- *Class Discussion*
- *Cooperative Project*
- *Group Discussion*
- *Rotating Reporters*
- *Stand and Share*

Background Information
The students have read or heard the story *Where the Wild Things Are* by Maurice Sendak.

Lesson Overview
"You have heard the story Where the Wild Things Are. You will help each other remember what happened at the rumpus. Your team will use this information to decide on a definition for the word rumpus."

Lesson Sequence

Class Discussion:

Ideas for Polite Ways to Give Suggestions
"As we decide on a team definition we are going to work on using Polite Suggestions. To make it easy to use Polite Suggestions let us make a list of some polite ways of offering and accepting ideas." List the student's suggestions which may be similar to the following:

"One idea is _____"
"Another idea is_____ "
"I like your idea."
"That is a good idea but_____"
"The best way to say it could be _____"
"Use these phrases when you make suggestions to the team. We shall check to see if teams remembered to use these polite statements while they worked together."

Group Discussion:

Gather Ideas
Students meet in teams of four and discuss what happened at a rumpus and use this information to suggest definitions of a rumpus.

Group Discussion:
Use of Polite Suggestions

After the teams have discussed for three or four minutes, give the Silent Signal. Read over the list of Polite Suggestions and have the teams discuss which statements their team used or if they had used a new polite statement. Remind them to continue using Polite Suggestions so they can share the statements they used during evaluation.

Group Discussion:
Decide on a Definition

"Now that the team has some ideas about a definition for a rumpus, decide on the best definition for your group. Practice saying the definition until everyone in the group knows the definition."

Stand and Share:
Share Team Definitions

Give each team a team number card. Then have all team members number off from one to four. All teams stand. Say a team number and a team member number. "Team four, person number three, share your team's definition." That team member says the definition for that team. "If any other teams had the same definition, please be seated. If your team's definition is different, please remain standing." Continue to call on teams until everyone is seated.

Group Discussion:
Use of Polite Statements

"Teams, discuss which polite statements each team used. Be sure everyone knows what these statements are."

Rotating Reporters:
Share Polite Statements

Call out a teammember number. The student on each team with that number, stands up. They are the reporters who go to the team with the next higher number (have them look at the team number cards) and tell that team the Polite Statements their team used. Example: The reporter from team # 1 goes to team #2 and tells team #2 the Polite Statements team #1 used.

Walk around and listen to the Polite Suggestions they are sharing. Have the reporters return to their own teams. "Teams, show thumbs up if the reporter shared a Polite Suggestion from his/her team. Compliment teams and repeat some of the Polite Suggestions you heard while the reporters were sharing.

Group Discussion:
Definition Refinement

If some of the definitions are not quite accurate or clear, the story can be read again while the teams collect information to improve or change their definitions.

Cooperative Project:
Teams Murals

Teams use their definition of a rumpus to make a description and mural of their own rumpus.

Rotating Reporters:
Debrief the Lesson

Use Rotating Reporters to find out how the students felt about the lessons. They discuss and report the answers to their questions.
• What did your team do to make it easy

Lorna Curran: *Lessons for Little Ones: Language Arts*©
Kagan Cooperative Learning • 1 (800) Wee Co-op

for you to share?
• Was it easy or hard for your team to use Polite Statements? Why?
• How did it feel to be the reporter for your group?
• Do you think the group could make a better definition if they heard the story again?

WorD WiZarDs

Lesson 25

• Literature
Any story with a
new or unfamiliar word

• Grade Level
1-2

• Type of Lesson
Reading Skills:
Learning Definitions

• Cognitive Objective
Students help each other learn vocabulary words so they can easily respond in a Word Wizard Game.

• Social Skills Objective
Active Listening

• Materials
Words and definitions written on the Vocabulary Study Card ditto sheets, Word Wizard Chips,
Word Wizard Certificates, Happy Talk Cards.

Structures
- Co-op Cards
- Numbered Heads
- Group Discussion
- Stand and Share
- Individuals Write

Lesson Overview

"Today we are going to help everyone on our team become a word wizard by learning words from our story and their meanings. Each team that teaches all their members well will have an easy time getting points in the Word Wizard Game we will play at the end of the lesson."

Lesson Sequence
Color-Coded Co-op Cards

Learn Vocabulary from a Story
A. Introduce the Words
Introduce the words by having them say the words and their meanings several times.

B. Preparation of Word Cards
Show the students how to cut, fold and glue the the flashcard sheet so that it becomes a set of flashcards for them to study. If everyone has the same words, the teacher can add the words to the vocabulary study card ditto before it is run off. If the words are different for each student, then they will need to be given a blank sheet to fill in. Have another student be your partner so you can model how two students can work together to get the job done quickly. Have the teams of four meet together and number from one to four. Students one and two are partners and so are students three and four. When they finish making the cards, they look at the words and their meanings to see if there are any questions they want to ask before they start the practice for the game.

C. Model Paired Practice

Have three students come and help you demonstrate how to do the paired practice. Number yourselves around the circle from one to four. Partners one and two study the words by having #1 be teacher and say the definition while #2 student supplies the word. At the same time partners three and four are doing the same thing. When all the words have been said, they reverse roles. During the second part of their practice, person one shows the word and person two tells the definition. Students three and four do the same. Students are to use a Praising Phrase after each correct answer. Have them read over the class Praise Chart to identify which of the phrases they can use as they work together.

D. Partners: Practice Co-op Cards

Go from group to group listening for Happy Talk. When you find a team that is using Happy Talk, you can stop the class for a moment to share how the group is using Happy Talk. When most of the partners have finished both parts of their practice, give the silent signal.

E. Partners Switch: Continue Co-op Cards Practice

Inform them that they will now practice with a new partner by having students one and four be partners and students two and three be partners. Have them repeat the practice with these partners so all team members are familiar with the words and definitions.

Individuals Write:

Use of Happy Talk

Give each team a stack of Happy Talk cards. Have everyone fill out one for each person on the team who told them a Happy Talk phrase while they were working together. They write the Happy Talk phrase they heard on the card. They turn the cards over when they are done.

Numbered Heads Together:

Play the Word Wizard Game

"Here is how we win Word Wizard Certificates in the Word Wizard Game. I might tell the class a definition. I will then call out a number. The person on each team who has that number stands to be ready to answer. Next I will call on one of these people to tell the word that goes with the definition. If I tell you a word, you tell the definition for that word."

Curran's Comments:

Call the students number first so that all students with that number will be alert and thinking of an answer. If you call the group name/number first, only the one team is alert. If you really want to keep everyone on their toes, call on any person to validate if the answer was correct or not, and state their reason for feeling the answer was correct or incorrect.

"If you give the correct answer, your group will receive a Word Wizard Chip. These chips will be counted and the total recorded on the Word Wizard Certificates." Play the game giving each team an equal number of chances to receive Word Wizard Chips.

Give Word Wizard Certificates

Collect and count up the Word Wizard Chips each team has won. Record that score on each team member's certificate. Pass out the certificates. Record team totals toward the class reward.

Group Discussion:

Share Happy Talk Cards

Have the students count up the number of Happy Talk certificates their team had. Teams report their score and total for a class score on using Happy Talk. Team-members give the Happy Talk cards to their partners so they can read the nice things they said while they were working together.

Stand and Share:

Debrief the Lesson

The teams discuss each of the questions listed below, agree on an answer and who will be the reporter. Everyone stands. Call on a group to share. That group and any other group with the same answer sits down. Continue until all ideas have been shared.

- How did the Color-Coded Co-op Card practice help your team earn Word Wizard Chips?
- What did your team do best today?
- What would help your team do even better next time?

Variations:

- The Happy Talk Cards can be collected and the teacher can share the comments with the class before the students give them to their partners.
- For Kindergarten, beginning first graders, or LEP students, make or have students make vocabulary cards with a word on one side and a picture on the other side.
- Each team can have a different set of words and each time the teams finish practicing they pass their set to the next team so they learn a new set of words.

Other Applications:

- Studying spelling words: Left side of the card: word, right side: blank
- Drill and practice of math facts: Left side: math fact, right side: math fact and answer
- Number Values: Left side: dots, right side: numbers

Extensions:

- Individuals or teams create stories, poems, and chants with the words they have studied.
- If each team studied different words, two teams get together and teach each other the words they learned, and then write stories using these new words.

Word Wizard Chips

Certificates

 **Word Wizard Certificate**

___ **Points**

For _____

 **Happy Talk Card**

_____

_____

_____

Lorna Curran: *Lessons for Little Ones: Language Arts*©

Kagan Cooperative Learning • 1 (800) Wee Co-op   **Lesson 25: 5**

Vocabulary Study Sheets

Write the vocabulary word on the left side and the
definition on the right side. Cut, fold and glue.

Lorna Curran: *Lessons for Little Ones: Language Arts*©
Kagan Cooperative Learning • 1 (800) Wee Co-op

Flash Card Sheet

Cut on the lines with arrows.

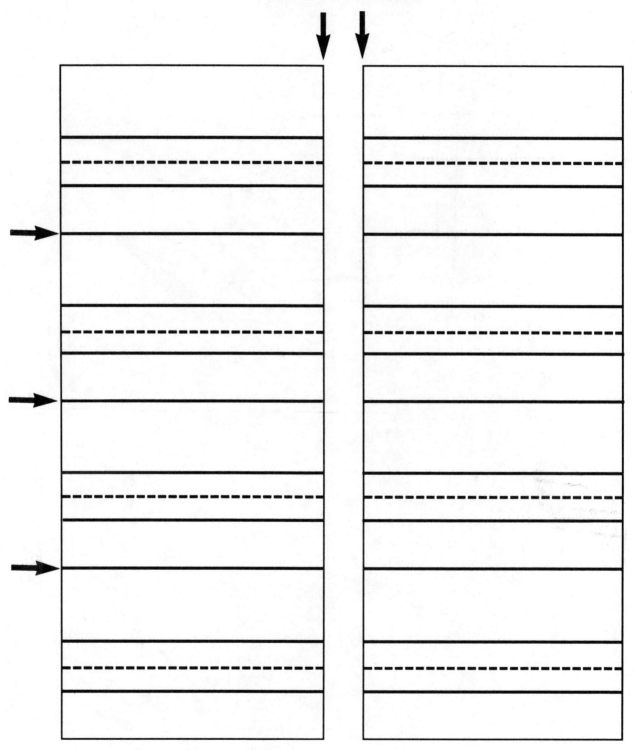

Lorna Curran: *Lessons for Little Ones: Language Arts*©
Kagan Cooperative Learning • 1 (800) Wee Co-op   **Lesson 25: 7**

Write & Share a Rhyming Pair

Lesson 26

• Literature

Tomie dePaola's Mother Goose
Read Aloud Rhymes

• Grade Level

K-1

• Type of Lesson

Reading Skills:
Rhyming Words

• Cognitive Objective

Students work together to create
lists of rhyming words.

• Social Skills Objective

Active Listening - Lean towards
the speaker

• Materials

Two pieces of paper and 2 pencils per group, chart paper for recording rhyming word families.

Structures
- *Numbered Heads*
- *Group Discussion*

Background Information

Students have heard stories and poems with rhyming words. Class discussions have led to the discovery of rhyming words within many of those stories. The students have used Active Listening many times so a reminder is all they need to remember to use Active Listening. Some suggested titles are: *Tomie dePaola's Mother Goose* by Tomie dePaola; *Read Aloud Rhymes* by Jack Prelutsky.

Lesson Overview

"In today's activity, I will say a word that rhymes with several words. Your team will think of at least two words that rhyme with the word I say. Someone in your group will be responsible for writing the words and someone will be responsible for sharing the words with

the class. As you work in your group and listen to the sharing, you are to be Active Listeners."

Lesson Sequence
Numbered Heads Together:

Think of Rhyming Words

A. Preparation for Group Discussion
The students meet in teams of four and number off within the group. Each team is given two pencils and two sheets of paper.

Group Discussion:

Think of Rhyming Words

"Students, I am going to say a word. Then everyone on the team needs to lean forward, use their Active Listening and help the team think of two words that rhyme with the word I say. Person #1 will write one of the words and Person #2 writes another word."

Lorna Curran: *Lessons for Little Ones: Language Arts*©
Kagan Cooperative Learning • 1 (800) Wee Co-op   **Lesson 26: 1**

Numbered Heads Together:

Share the Words

"Give the papers to students #3 and #4. As I call your team, students #3 and #4 will read the words on the paper even if another team has already said the word." Record the words they share to make Rhyming Word Family Charts.

Numbered Heads Together:

Use of Active Listening

Have the teams discuss whether everyone on the team leaned in to show they were using Active Listening. Also have them discuss if they did anything else to show that they were good listeners. "I am going to say a number. The person on each team with that number please stand. When I call on your team, tell if your team leaned toward each other and showed Active Listening." Compliment teams for remembering to lean in towards each other and remembering other parts of Active Listening.

Numbered Heads Together:

Add to Rhyming Word List

Continue to create several lists of rhyming words. Reverse the roles each time a new word is given. Every time person #1 and #2 write, persons #3 and #4 read. Every time persons #3 and #4 write, persons #1 and #2 read. If most or all the teams contribute rhyming words, the objective was met. If the students had difficulties providing rhyming words, do the lesson again after hearing many more rhyming stories and poems.

Group Discussion:

Debrief the Lesson

Find out how the students felt about doing the lesson by allowing groups to discuss the following questions:

- What did your team do that helped you?
- What did your team do to show Active Listening?
- What did your team do to make it easy for the person who was writing rhyming words for the team?

Other Applications:

- Create lists of synonyms.
- Find replacements for over-used common words like "good" or "said".
- Develop a list of character traits for a storybook character.

Sample Rhyming Word Family Chart

AT
CAT
FAT
MAT
SAT
RAT
CHAT
HAT
SPLAT

Rhyming Roundtable

• Literature

Sheep In A Jeep
A Time To Rhyme With Calico Cat
Jamberry

• Grade Level

1-2

• Type of Lesson

Reading Skills: Rhyming Words

• Cognitive Objective

Teams of students work together to create Rhyming Word Families.

• Social Skills Objective

Quiet Voices, Quick Work

• Materials

Rhyming Word Family sheets, 1 per team (sample included), one pencil per group.

Structures

• *Group Discussion*
• *Numbered Heads*
• *Rotating Reporter*
• *Roundtable*

Background Information

Students have heard many stories with rhyming words such as those listed in the materials section of this lesson. They have had opportunities to identify rhyming words within these stories. They have had some experience making Rhyming Word Family lists as a total class. Some suggested titles are: *Sheep In A Jeep* by Nancy Shaw; *A Time To Rhyme With Calico Cat* by Donald Charles; *Jamberry* by Bruce Degen.

Lesson Overview

"Teams you will work together to think of words that belong in the same rhyming family as the word written at the top of your rhyming word family sheet. Work quietly and quickly to write a rhyming word and then pass the paper

to the next team member. Do this until time is called".

Lesson Sequence

Roundtable:

Preparation for Roundtable

Students meet in teams of three or four. Each team is given a Rhyming Word Family sheet and a pencil. They number themselves around the group so they know which team member writes first, second, third, and fourth.

Group Discussion/ Roundtable:

Gather Rhyming Words

The team decides on a rhyming word to add to their sheet. Person #1 writes the word and passes the sheet to person #2. The group decides on another word for person #2 to write and the paper passes to person #3. Continue until all mem-

---

bers of all teams have had at least one turn.

Rotating Reporter:

Passing Quickly and Quietly

Have the groups decide what they are doing to help each other work quickly and quietly. Have person #1 from each team be ready to go tell one or more other teams what their team has done to help each other. Show the students which teams they will move to, then when the command is given, they move to that team to tell them how the group helped each other. Listen as these students talk to the other teams. Share with the class some of the suggestions you heard. Give the groups a couple of minutes to decide if any of these suggestions would help their team work even better.

Roundtable:

Gathering Rhyming Words

Have the students continue the process of gathering rhyming words until time is called in about ten minutes.

Numbered Heads Together:

Share Rhyming Families

Have the teams practice reading the Rhyming Family Word sheets until everyone on the team can read all the words on the sheet. Have a box of number cards with as many numbers as there are members on the teams. Pull out a number card each time you call on a team and the person with that number will read the Rhyming Word Family sheet to the class.

Finger Evaluation/ Group Discussion:

Use of Quick Passing and Working Quietly

Have the teams count up how many rhyming words they have on their sheet. Any teams that have at least ten words on the sheet, give a thumbs up signal (you decide what would be an appropriate number of words for your class). The teams discuss whether their group used quiet voices while they worked together. If the team has a good reason for thinking their team used quiet voices while they worked together, they have person #2 make a happy face of the back of the Rhyming Word Family sheet. Person #3 will be ready to write down or tell the reason for the happy face. If the team felt they didn't use quiet voices, person #2 draws a light bulb. Person #3 writes down ideas to help the team do a better job next time.

Group/Class Discussion:

Debrief the Lesson

Find out how the teams felt about the lesson by discussing the following questions.

- ✏ "What worked well for your team as you collected words for the rhyming families?"
- ✏ "What did your team do so everyone would remember to work quietly?"
- ✏ "What suggestions helped your team work quickly and quietly ?"
- ✏ "What are some other things that could have helped your team work even better?"

Variations:

- Each team can have the same word on their Rhyming Word Family sheet.
- Each team can have a word for a different Rhyming Word Family.
- Each team member could have a different Rhyming Word sheet which they would pass to each other for a Simultaneous Roundtable.
- Alternate verbs. The teacher says a verb and the students think of synonyms.
- Alternate nouns. The teacher says a noun and the students think of synonyms.
- The teacher says one of the facts in a number family and the students think of all the other members of that number family.

Extensions:

- Students use the Rhyming Word Family sheets to write a team poem.
- Write team poetry books where each team member uses one of the Rhyming Word Family sheets to help him write at least one poem that will be put in the team poetry book. The team members support each other and help them gain ideas.
- Teams investigate poems to discover the rhyming words used. They can make their own Rhyming Word Families resource books.

Rhyming Word Family Sheet

cat

Rhyming Word Family Sheet

tall

pig

bee

king

bed

Retell Rosie

Lesson 28

• Literature

Rosie's Walk

• Grade Level
K-1

• Type of Lesson
Writing Skills: Recreate and read a story

• Cognitive Objective
Teams make books that retell a story to use for storytelling.

• Social Skills Objective
Happy Talk (Compliments)

• Materials

Crayons, pencils, scissors, glue, one large piece of white construction paper per group, one colored piece of paper per group, six 3"x4" pieces of white construction paper per group, an envelope of sentence strips that tell where Rosie walked, and a footprint master per group.

- **Class Discussion**
- **Cooperative Project**
- **Group Discussion**
- **Rotating Reporters**
- **Roundrobin**
- **Team I-O Circle**

Structures

Background Information

The class has heard or read the story *Rosie's Walk* by Pat Hutchins several times so they are familiar with the places Rosie went on her walk.

Lesson Overview

"We heard the story Rosie's Walk several times. You know the story so well you will be able to use the books we make to tell the story to others. When we are done making the pages for the team book, the teammembers will compliment each other on how well they worked."

Lesson Sequence

Class Discussion:

Think of Compliments
"Before we start, let's think of some compliments we can give out teammembers." Write down the students' suggestions which may be similar to the following: "Your picture is neat." "Rosie is cute." "Thank you for sharing the crayons with me."

Cooperative Project:

Team Story Books
A. Preparation for Book Making
Students work in teams of six. Each team is given crayons, pencils, 6 pieces of white construction paper, one colored piece of

construction paper with the title ROSIE'S WALK written across the top, six pieces of 3"x4" white construction paper, and an envelope of sentence strips that tell where Rosie walked (see 28:3).

B. Group Discussion: Read and Assign Book Page Strips

"Each teammember is to take from the envelope one of the sentence strips that tells where Rosie walked. This strip tells you which part of the story you will be drawing and writing about. Help each other read the sentence strips so everyone knows which part of the story they are to do."

C. Draw an Illustration

"After everyone knows what their sentence strip says, use the large white paper and crayons to draw Rosie in the place your sentence strip describes. Leave space at the top to write your sentence."

D. Group Discussion: Check for Compliments

Have the teams discuss any compliments they gave. Have a few students share compliments they heard. "Remember to use compliments as your team adds sentences, footprints and author cards to complete the book."

E. Write the Sentence

"When you finish the picture, take a pencil and write the sentence that tells where Rosie is. Look at the sentence strip if you need help." Kindergarten students can glue the sentence strip on the picture if they are not yet comfortable writing.

F. Add Footprints

"When you finish your picture and sentence, color the footprints, cut them out, and glue them on to the picture to show where Rosie walked. For example, if you did the picture that shows the sentence, 'Rosie walked around the pond,' you would glue the footprints so they look like they go around the pond."

Curran's Comments:

I like to carve the footprint shape onto potatoes so students can potato print the footprints on their pictures with brown tempera paint. I either have them come to a separate table to paint, or I take a pie pan containing a sponge covered with brown tempera paint to each team as they are ready for it.

G. Make Author Cards

"Students, after you add the footprints, while your team's pictures are drying, take one of the small white papers and draw a picture of yourself to make an author card. Write your name on your card. Then each of the teammembers glues their author cards onto the colored construction paper book cover underneath the title ROSIE'S WALK."

H. Group Discussion: Arrange Book Pages in Correct Order

"When your group has finished the book cover, help each other pile the pictures in the order in which they happened in the story. Put the cover on top of the pile. Everyone raise your hands to let me know when your team is done. I will come and check the order of the pages and staple it together."

Team In-Outside Circle/ Roundrobin
Teams Tell Their Stories
"While the other students are finishing their books, your team will sit in a circle and use the book to help your group practice telling the story." Then use Inside-Outside Circle to let teams share their books. Teams can use Roundrobin as they read their story to each new team. Remember to compliment each team after they "read" their story.

Group Discussion:
Remember Compliments Given
Again the teams are given a few minutes to remember the compliments they received. "Teams, choose three compliments you want to share with another team. Practice saying those compliments so the whole team can say them."

Rotating Reporters:
Share Compliments
"Now Rotating Reporters will share the compliments with another team. Half of each team will be moving to another team to form sharing groups. Take a minute and number yourselves from 1 to 6. Team members 1, 2, and 3 stay where you are. Teammembers 4, 5, and 6 stand. You are the reporters and you will move to the group I point out to you. When you get to the new group show Active Listening." Monitor that they move in the right direction. "Now that you are in your sharing groups, persons 1, 2, and 3 will each tell a compliment their team used. Then persons 4, 5, and 6 will each tell a compliment

their team used." Listen to the Reporters as they share and write down some of the compliments you hear them sharing with each other. "Teammembers 4, 5, and 6 now move to the next group. Continue rotating and sharing as many times as you desire."

Finger Evaluation:
Evaluate Use of Compliments
"Sharing groups that heard everyone tell a compliment, show thumbs up." Praise or reward according to how many thumb signals are given. Validate by sharing the compliments you heard while they were sharing.

Rotating Reporters:
Debrief the Lesson Using Rotating Reporters
Find out how the teams felt about the lesson by letting them discuss some of the following questions. Choose a reporter and send this reporter to anoth-

Rosie's Walk Sentence Strips

across the yard
around the pond
over the haystack
past the mill
through the fence
under the beehive

er group to share their answer. Send a different reporter for each new question.

What did your team do that made it easy to:

- Read the sentence to your team?
- Get help defining a word in a sentence?
- Receive and give compliments?
- What made it easy to share your book with an other team?

Other Applications:

- Use the story *Hattie and the Fox* by Mem Fox. The team members would illustrate what the different characters said.

- Use the story *The Cock, The Mouse, And The Little Red Hen* by Lorinda Cauley. Groups of three illustrate what each animal in the story said.
- Use the story *Cookies' Week* by Cindy Ward. Groups of six tell what happened to Cookie on each of the days but Sunday. Each person could then give their own ideas of what will happen on Sunday, so the story would have six possible endings.

Footprint Patterns

Footprint Patterns

Colorful Chameleons

Lesson 29

- **Grade Level**

    K-1

- **Literature**

    The Mixed-Up Chameleon
    A Color Of His Own

- **Type of Lesson**

    Writing Skills: Color
    Categories/ Descriptive Words

- **Cognitive Objective**

    Students will brainstorm things that
    are a certain color and use that
    information to make a group book.

- **Social Skills Objective**

    Everyone Participates

- **Materials**

    Post-its and small papers for each student, color signs, Chameleon ditto for each student, construction paper for each student's background picture, one construction paper per group for the book's cover, crayons, pencils, scissors, glue, large paper for brainstorming, idea chips, Participation Pat cut outs.

- *Corners*
- *Team 9-0 Circle*
- *Roundrobin*
- *Group Discussion*
- *Cooperative Project*

Structures

Background Information

Students have heard or read *A Color Of His Own* by Leo Lionni. They know the color names and will have had opportunities to categorize objects into color groups. They have talked about the fact that Chameleons camouflage themselves by changing color so they match the color of the things around them. Another suggested titles is: *The Mixed-Up Chameleon* by Eric Carle.

Lesson Overview

"Today you will be working together to make Chameleon books. Groups think of objects that Chameleons could sit on so that in your group's book all the Chameleons will be camouflaged. As groups work, we want to encourage everyone to participate by sharing ideas and creating a page for the group book."

Lesson Sequence

Ideas for Encouraging Statements

"Let's think about some things we can say to encourage members of our group to contribute ideas." Write down the ideas they contribute on an Encouraging Statement Chart. Some things you could write on the chart would be:
"What do you think _____?"
"Do you have an idea _____?"
"What is your idea _____?"
"(name)_____ help us get ideas."

Corners

A. Select a Color

Give each student a Post-it. "In a few minutes, you will be coloring a picture of a Chameleon. Think what color you

---

would like your Chameleon to be and color the Post-it that color."

B. Form Corners Groups
Hang signs, each made of one of the eight basic colors. Put each color sign in a different section of the room. These signs designate where the color groups will meet. "Students put on your Post-it and move to the sign that is the same color as your Post-it."

C. Materials for Corners Groups
Give each group a large piece of paper for a brainstorm sheet, a container of the correct color crayons for their group, and a box of Idea Chips.

D. Directions for Corners Groups
Give the Silent Signal. "Your group is to brainstorm all the things your Chameleon could sit on so that he will be camouflaged. For example, the green group will brainstorm green things for the Chameleon to sit on, the blue group will brainstorm blue things."

Curran's Comments:
Groups of four to six students works well with this lesson. If there are more than six students at a particular color group, divide that group into smaller groups.

E. Idea Chips: Contribute Ideas for Brainstorm sheet
Make sure each person in the group has two Idea Chips. As each person in the group shares an idea about what the Chameleon could sit on, they will put one of their Idea Chips in the box, and then write the word or draw a picture for that object on the brainstorm sheet.

"When you have used both of your Idea Chips, you may not give any more ideas until everyone in the group has used all their chips. Then you may give as many ideas as you want."

Group Discussion:
Choose an Item
"After everyone in the group has given at least two ideas, each person in the group can choose a different item for their Chameleon to sit on. As someone chooses an idea, they write their name on the brainstorm sheet right next to that item. When everyone in the group has chosen what they will draw, all of you are to raise your hands."

Participation Pat:
Individual Recognition
As groups of students raise their hands, go to their team, and count the Idea Chips in the box to be sure everyone has contributed two ideas. Check the brainstorm sheet to see that each group member has chosen a different item to draw. If everyone in the group has done their part, the teammembers give themselves a pat on the back and sign their names on a "Participation Pat" cut out which is then glued to the bottom of the Encouraging Statements Chart.

Cooperative Project:
Make Illustration
Each student is given a Chameleon ditto and background paper. "On this paper you will draw a picture which includes the object you choose for the Chameleon to sit on. Then color and cut out the Chameleon and glue it in the right place on your picture."

B. Describe the Picture

The students will then add a sentence that describes their Chameleon. They could write a sentence such as: "The purple Chameleon is sitting on a purple flower." Third grade students could add additional descriptive words. Kindergarten students might need the sentence pre-written so all they need to write are the words which are unique to their own sentence. "The _____ Chameleon is sitting on a _____ _____." While students are drawing, you can circulate, writing on a small paper the words each students will write to fill in the blanks.

C. Assembling and Reads the Books

The pages for each group are stapled together including a cover page. The group practices reading the book so they are ready to share it. Then they sign their names on the cover and add a picture or design if there is time.

Team I-O Circle/ Roundrobin:

Teams Read Books to Other Teams

Teams form a Team Inside-Outside Circle so the groups can read their books to each other. Teams are rotated so all students have many opportunities to read their stories. Roundrobin is used within the teams so all students read.

Roundrobin:

Debrief the Lesson

Find out how the teams felt about the lesson by having teammembers take turns discussing the following questions with each other.

- How did the group help you get ideas for your part of the story?

- How did your team help each other as you worked together to make your book?
- Was it easy or hard for your team to make this book? Why?
- Was it easy or hard for your team to share their book? Why?

Extensions:

- Write additional pages for the group books that explain what happens to the Chameleons as they sit on their objects. Tell what they see, hear, and feel while they are sitting in those places.
- To make sure each student reads the group's whole book to another team, use Rotating Reporting, which means a different teammember reads the book each time the book is read to a new team.
- Write a story about your Chameleon getting loose in your bedroom. Think of all the places he could hide and what colors he would become while he was there. Tell all about his adventure and how you would finally catch him.

Applications to Other Lionni books:

- *Frederick* - Each corner group represents a color Frederick thought about. They would brainstorm and then make a booklet about all the things of each color that Frederick could think about.
- *Fish Is Fish* - The students could choose a creature other than a fish to go off in the world and return to describe all the animals it sees. Students who choose the same animal would become the corner groups. These groups would brainstorm the types of things their animal had to describe to his friends.

Variations:

- This can become a Jigsaw lesson where the corner groups become expert groups. The team would have each member choose a different color to put on their Post-it. This would put each teammember in a different expert group. Each person in the group would make a brainstorm sheet which includes all the ideas in their group. They would then take their brainstorm sheet back to their team. The team would decide which item from the brainstorm sheet would be drawn by that member for the team book. Teams would then end up with multi-colored books, one color per teammember.

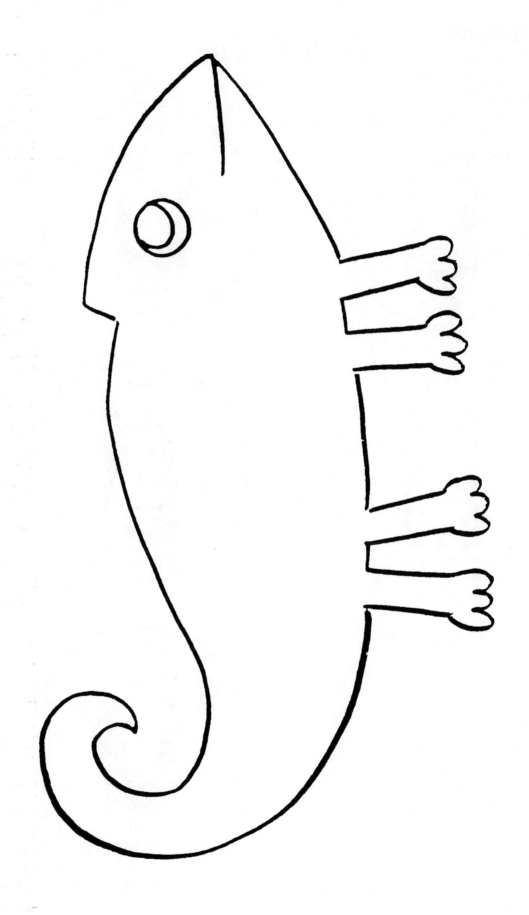

Idea Chips

Participation Pat Outline

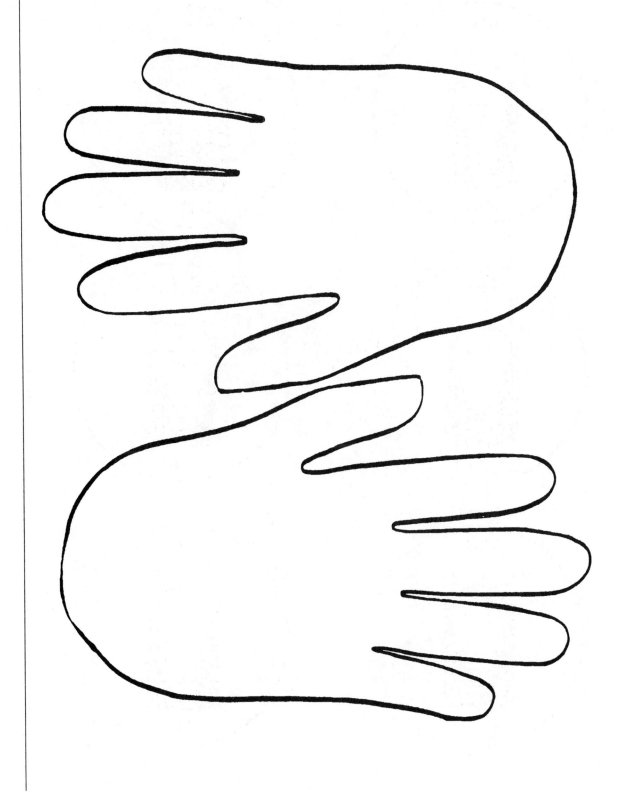

Colorful Chants

• Literature

Color Seems
Snoopy's Book of Color
Hailstones & Halibut Bones
Brown Bear, Brown Bear,
What Do You See

• Grade Level

K-1

• Type of Lesson

Writing Skills

• Cognitive Objective

Groups of students create a color
chant using pictures and words.

• Social Skills Objective

Accepting Suggestions Politely,
Everyone Participates

• Materials

Chant Strips, tape, and background paper.

Structures

- *Class Discussion*
- *Cooperative Project*
- *Group Discussion*
- *Inside-Outside Circle*

Background Information

The students have learned to name the colors, identify objects of different colors, and classify objects by color. They have made a collage for each basic color and have brainstormed a picture chart for each color. Suggested titles are: *Brown Bear, Brown Bear, What Do You See* by Bill Martin; *Hailstones & Halibut Bones* by Leonard Weisgard; *Color Seems* by Ima Haskins; *Snoopy's Book of Color* by Charles Shultz.

Lesson Overview

"Students today we are going to work in groups and use the ideas on our picture charts to write chants about colors. While we work, we will ask our teammembers for suggestions and accept them politely. The team will practice saying the chant and read it to the class."

Lesson Sequence

Class Discussion:

Brainstorm Polite Statements
Before the teams start working on their chants, make a chart as the students brainstorm some polite statements they can make to their teammembers for giving them suggestions for their color. Examples could be:

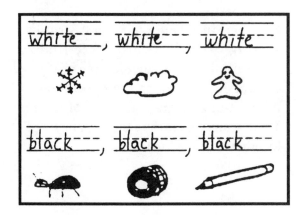

- Those were good ideas.
- I like your ideas.
- Thanks, that will help me.

A. Share A Sample Chant
The teacher shows and reads a color chant such as the following.

B. Model Making A Chant
Choose a couple of students to work with you to demonstrate how to make a chant. Go through the following steps as you make your chant:

C. Group Discussion: Decide Colors For Chant
The team decides what colors to use in their chant. Use as many colors as there are people on the team. Each teammember chooses one of the colors to write about in the chant.

D. Group Discussion: Brainstorm Objects for Each Color
Each person asks their teammembers for ideas of objects that could be that color. "What things can you think of that are red?" "Strawberries." "Tomatoes." "Stop signs." "Hearts." "Roses." Make a polite statement to your teammembers for the suggestions they gave you. "Thank you for the ideas."

E. Group Discussion: Make and Arrange Chant Strips
Each person fills in their chant strip by writing the color word three times. Underneath they draw pictures of three or four ideas they or their teammates thought of and draw pictures of them. The teammembers tape their chant strips together to make the team chant.

Group Discussion:
Recognize Polite Suggestions
When most of the teams have finished the brainstorming, show the Silent Signal. Ask the groups to remember the polite statements their teammembers used. Have them share at least one polite statement they heard in their team. Recognize teams as they share statements with the class.

Cooperative Project:
Practice the Chant
As soon as the teams have their chants taped together, they practice saying the chant. Everyone must participate in the sharing of the chant.

Team I-O Circle:
Share the Chants
Form a Team Inside-Outside Circle. Each team has a chance to share their chant several times as they rotate from one team to the next.

Inside-Outside Circle:
Debrief the Lesson
Have teams share with each other what worked best for them today. They can also discuss what made this activity fun to do.

Other Applications:
- Number Chants. Each person on the team takes a different number, writes the number word three times, and draws things that are always found with that many in a set.

- **Weekday Chants.** Each student on the team takes a different day of the week, writes the number word three times, and draws things that happen on that day of the week.
- **Sports/Games.** Each student on the team chooses a different sport or game, writes the name of the sport or game three times and then writes words associated with that game or sport.

Variations

- First grade students write words for the objects instead of drawing pictures.
- Second grade students write a sentence that tells about the objects.
- Second grade students write two sentences about the objects and the sentences must rhyme.

Chant Strips

_____

-------------------------------,

_____

-------------------------------,

_____

-------------------------------,

_____

-------------------------------,

Sweet Similes

• Literature
Stories with similes

• Grade Level
K-1

• Type of Lesson
Writing Skills: Similes

• Cognitive Objective
Students think of similes for colors.

• Social Skills Objective
Quiet Voices

• Materials
Sweet Simile ditto (included), pencils, crayons, glue, Super Silent Sixes (included), book.

Structures
• **Cooperative Project**
• **Group Discussion**
• **Partners**
• **Pair I-O Circle**
• **Think-Pair-Share**

Background Information
Students have had instruction on what similes are. They have practiced making similes as a class.

Lesson Overview
"Today you and a partner will be thinking of similes for things that are a certain color. As you work together to think of and write down similes, you will concentrate on using Six-Inch Voices so your work does not disturb other partners."

Lesson Sequence
Review Six-Inch Voices
"Remember when you use a Six-Inch Voice, you need to lean in towards your partner and have good eye contact with that person as he/she speaks."

Cooperative Project:
Make Color Similes
A. Preparation for Similes
Divide the class into partners. Give each pair a Sweet Simile paper, pencils, crayons, one white card, and one red card. "One of you sign the white card and the other sign the red card."

B. Assigning Tasks
"Today's similes are telling how red or how white some thing would be. Together you will think of things that are red or white to write on the simile paper. The person who signed the red card will write down the red similes, for example he might write down the word tomato to make the simile, 'as red as a tomato.' The person who signed the white card will write down the ideas for the white similes; for example she might write down snow to make the simile, 'as white as snow.' Talk the ideas over and spell the

words the best way you can. If you are really puzzled, both of you raise your hands and I will come to help you. Remember to use Six-Inch voices as we will be taking a vote in a few minutes to see how well we think we are doing in using quiet voices that do not disturb the people around us. I will give you the Silent Signal in about five minutes."

Curran's Comments:

Kindergarten and first grade students who are not yet comfortable writing, will enjoy the activity if they can draw the things that are white or red.

Partners:

Think of and Write Similes

Observe the use of Six-Inch Voices and help with any spelling problems. After five minutes ask for the Silent Signal. Notice how much they have done so you will know how much more time they will need to finish the job.

Finger Evaluation:

Check for Six-Inch Voices

"Now that you have worked for five minutes, let's check on our use of Six-Inch Voices. If the partners around you used quiet voices so you could hardly hear them, show the thumbs up signal." Compliment them for a job well done, and/or encourage them to think more about using the Six-Inch Voices. "Continue to use Six-Inch Voices as you have about ten minutes more to finish writing the similes. If you finish early,

think of how you would use each of the similes in a sentence."

Group Discussion:

Practice the Similes

"I will give you a few minutes to practice saying your similes and then lightly color in the Sweet Similes paper. Be sure to color so that the words will still show."

Group Discussion:

Recognition of Six-Inch Voices

"We are going to give each of the partners who used Six-Inch Voices a Super Silent Six. I am going to show each of you which partners you will think about to see if their voices were so quiet that they should have a Super Silent Six." Give each pair of students a different set of partners to evaluate for silent voices. Let them discuss how well that set of partners did. "If both of you feel the partners should have a Super Silent Six, the red person from your pair will come and get a Super Silent Six to take to the partners you were to evaluate. They will glue the Super Silent Six to their sweet simile paper." Count the Super Silent Sixes and praise and or reward accordingly.

Partners Inside-Outside Circle:

Read the Sweet Similes

Put two sets of partners together, one pair in an inner circle, and one pair in an outer circle, so they can read their sweet similes to each other. Then have the partners in the inner circle rotate to the next partner group to share. Rotate and share several times.

Think-Pair-Share:

Debrief the Lesson

To find out how the students felt about the lesson, have partners discuss and share some of the following questions.

- What made it easy for you and your partner to think of similies and write them down.
- How did you help each other remember to use the six-inch voice?
- What made it easy and hard to read your simile to another group?

Extensions:

- Partners now write sentences using the similes they created.
- Partners exchange similes and create sentences for those similes.
- Partners or individuals write a story in which they use at least two if the similes from their sweet similes paper.

Other Applications:

Any colors, sizes, shapes, and feelings can be used to create similes.

Sweet Similes

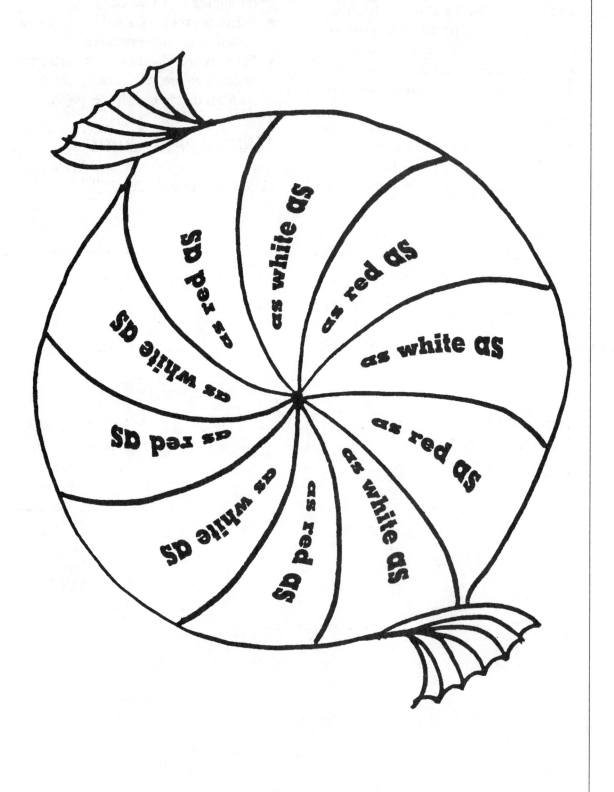

Super Silent Six

Lorna Curran: *Lessons for Little Ones: Language Arts*©
Kagan Cooperative Learning • 1 (800) Wee Co-op

Lesson 31: 5

Paint Pallet Prose

Lesson 32

• Literature

Mr. Rabbit and the Lovely Present
Who Said Red?
Green Says Go
If You Take a Paintbrush
Planting a Rainbow

• Grade Level

K-2

• Type of Lesson

Writing Skills: Color Poetry

• Cognitive Objective

Students work together to
create a color poem.

• Social Skills Objective

Happy Talk (Show Appreciation)

• Materials

Color lists, poem frame ditto, construction paper, colored pens and glue.

- **Class Discussion**
- **Cooperative Project**
- **Group Discussion**
- **Team I-O Circle**
- **Rotating Reporters**

Structures

Background Information

Students have learned the names of the basic colors. They have categorized objects, and/or have made lists of objects that are a particular color. They can use Lesson 23: Brain-storming Blue to make their lists. Some suggested titles are: *Mr. Rabbit and the Lovely Present* by Charlote Zolotow; *Who Said Red?* by Mary Serfozo; *Green Says Go* by Ed Emberley; *If You Take a Paintbrush* by Fulvio Testa; and *Planting a Rainbow* by Lois Ehlert.

Lesson Overview

"In this lesson we are going to use the ideas we brainstormed for each color to make color poems. Each team will follow the form used in a sample poem that I will write for you. Then your team can make a poem about the color that is assigned to your team. You will use Happy Talk as you work together."

Lesson Sequence

Class Discussion:

Use of Happy Talk

"What kinds of Happy Talk could be used as you create your poem? I'll write them down so they will be ready for you to use as you work together. "
"That is a good idea."
"I like your idea."
"You write neatly."
"You used just a little glue."

List quite a few of the Happy Talk statements they tell you. Remind them to use these and other Happy Talk statements as they work together so each of the team members can receive a compliment from their team at the end of the lesson.

Cooperative Project:

Create a Color Poem

A. Make a Sample Poem

To demonstrate how to make a color poem, use a color that will not be assigned to the teams. Write each line of the poem on a separate sentence strip.

White

White is a daisy.

White is a lamb.

White are the snowflakes.

White are the clouds up in the sky.

I love white.

B. Learn the Formula for the Poem

"To make this poem, someone writes the color and that becomes the title of your poem. Each teammember writes a sentence about your team's color. The first sentence tells about one object that is your color (White is a daisy). The second sentence tells about another object that is your color (White is a lamb). The third sentence tells about something there are several of (White are the snowflakes). The fourth sentence tells about something there are several of and tells where those things are found (White are the clouds up in the sky). Finally someone on the team finishes the poem by writing "I love _____."

C. Preparation for Writing the Poem

Teams are assigned their color and are given pens of that color for writing the poem. They are given sentence strips and a piece of construction paper to glue the sentence strips on to make the poem.

D. Group Discussion: Teams Plan and Write the Poem

Teammembers look at the color lists and decide on two singular objects for the first two lines of the poem and two plural objects for the second two lines of the poem. They choose a different teammate to write the title and each of the sentences of the poem. They each write their sentence on a sentence strip. The title and last line are also written. The strips are laid out in the correct order. Teammates glue their strips onto the construction paper.

Group Discussion:

Compliment Happy Talk

Help the students decide how they can compliment their team members for using Happy Talk. Some of their ideas may be: "I like it when you said, 'Good job." "Thank you for telling me I had a good idea." You told us our writing is neat. That was nice." Give the team members a few minutes to thank each other for using Happy Talk.

Team In-Outside Circle:

Share Poems

The teams are given several minutes to plan how they want to share their poem. Then they practice saying the poem. Everyone participates in presenting the poem several times as they rotate in Team Inside-Outside Circle.

Rotating Reporters:

Debrief the Lesson

Teams stay in their circle and discuss the following questions. They send a reporter out to the next team in their circle to share the answer to the first question and another reporter to the second team away to show the answer to the second question.

* What made it easy for your team to plan and make their poem?

- How did you decide the way you would show your poem?
- Should your team use the same procedure when you make another poem or would another way work better for you? Explain.
- How did you feel when the team shared the poem?
- How did it feel when someone complimented you for using Happy Talk?

Extensions:

- Teams practice reading their poem until everyone is comfortable reading it. Teams Share is used so teams teach another team how to read their poem.
- The teams make a neat copy of their poem along with accompanying illustrations to have on the bulletin board or make into a class book.
- After hearing poems about several colors as teams share their poems with each other, each team uses the ideas they heard to write a poem about several different colors. Each team has it's own color poetry book.
- Teach the students colors such as burgundy, aqua, beige, chartreuse. The teams try making poems for the unusual colors.

Variations:

- For first grade or advanced Kindergarten students, use the lined poem frame so they have to write only the color and name of the object that goes in each sentence.
- Kindergarten students can use the unlined poem frame so they only need to write the color and then can draw a picture of the object in each sentence.
- Each poem could include several colors by having each team member responsible for a different color.

Unlined Poem Frame

_____

_____ is a

_____

_____ is a

_____

_____ are the

_____

_____ are the

       _____

   I Love _____

Lined Poem Frame

_____   _____

-------------------------------   -------------------------------

_____ is a _____

_____   _____

-------------------------------   -------------------------------

_____ is a _____

_____   _____

-------------------------------   -------------------------------

_____ are the _____

_____   _____

-------------------------------   -------------------------------

_____ are the _____

_____

I Love _____

Lorna Curran: _Lessons for Little Ones: Language Arts_©

Kagan Cooperative Learning • 1 (800) Wee Co-op   **Lesson 32: 5**

Talking Trees

• Literature

The Alphabet Tree

• Grade Level

1-2

• Type of Lesson

Writing Skills: Sentence Writing

• Cognitive Objective

Students work together to create a tree with a sentence containing a message for the president.

• Social Skills Objective

Happy Talk

• Materials

Ditto sheets of leaves, pens or pencil to write words, large paper for the tree, crayons, scissors, and glue.

• Cooperative Project
• Class Discussion
• Group Discussion
• Teams Share
• Roundtable
• Rotating Reporters

Structures

Background Information

Students have heard or read the story *The Alphabet Tree* by Leo Lionni. The class has discussed who the president is, what his job is, and some issues that would be important to write to the president about.

Lesson Overview

"Your team is going to make an alphabet tree with a message for the president. Your team will think of a message, write the words for the message on leaves, cut out the leaves, and glue them to a tree you draw. While you work together, you will use Happy Talk to compliment each other on nice things that are said and done." Show students the sample tree provided at the end of the lesson.

Lesson Sequence

Class Discussion:

Ideas for Happy Talk

"Because you are to use Happy Talk while you make the alphabet tree, let's think of some compliments you could give each other as you work together." Write down the suggestions the students make which may be similar to these. "That's a good idea." "Good message." "Good cutting." "That's neat writing." "That's a terrific tree we made!"

Roundtable:

Create a Message

A. Group Discussion: Choose Several Messages

Students meet in teams of four. "Your team will think of several messages that could be sent to the president. Choose the one your team likes best. Say it together several times so you won't forget your sentence. When you finish, start cutting out your four leaves until I give the silent signal. Remember to use Happy Talk."

Teams Share:
Check for Use of Happy Talk

Give the teams a minute to decide if they used Happy Talk. Have the teams that did use Happy Talk share a statement with the team next to them. Praise or reward them for use of Happy Talk. Remind them to continue using Happy Talk and to try to use some different Happy Talk statements.

C. Preparation for Alphabet Tree

Teams number off so each team member has a number. The team is given a large background paper, crayons, and a bottle of glue. Each team member receives a strip of four leaves, a pair of scissors, and a pencil.

D. Roundtable: Write the Sentence

"Now your team will share the responsibility of writing the sentence by having Person #1 write the first word of the sentence on one of their leaves, Person #2 writes the second word of the sentence on one of their leaves, and so on until all

---

Curran's Comments:

I usually run off extra pieces because some groups finish early and can use their extra time making additional pieces which they can add to their project. It's what I call a "Sponge Activity" because the extra cutting soaks up their extra time. Sometimes in this activity, a fast team will create an additional sentence to use up their extra leaves.

---

the words of the sentence are written on the leaves. There may be enough words in the sentence so some of the people on the team may have more than one leaf with a word on it. Then continue cutting out all your leaves. If your team has time to cut out extra leaves, there are more available. I'll be listening for Happy Talk." As the students work, walk around listening and writing down Happy Talk statements that you hear.

Cooperative Project:
Construct the Tree

"Your team now needs to make the tree. First share drawing the sky, a tree trunk, and branches. Then arrange the leaves on the tree. Be sure the words are in the right order so the sentence can be read. Then everyone helps glue the leaves on to the tree. I am hearing a lot of Happy Talk. Keep up the good job."

Group Discussion:
Recall the Use of Happy Talk

Pass out to each team, a HAPPY TALK CARD. "Your team will have about five minutes to remember and write down at least two Happy Talk statements your team used. Then Person #2 will read these statements to another team when I give the silent signal."

Rotating Reporters:
Share Happy Talk Statements

Give the Silent Signal. Let the #2 person on each team know which team they will go to to share Happy Talk statements. "Would person #2 from each team now go to the team assigned to you and read two of your teams Happy Talk statements. Then hand the HAPPY TALK

Lorna Curran: *Lessons for Little Ones: Language Arts*©

CARD to person #3 on that team. Person #3 raise your hand so we know who you are."

Group Discussion:

Evaluate Use of Happy Talk

"If your team did hear two Happy Talk statements, person #3 will draw a happy face at the bottom of the HAPPY TALK CARD. Give the card back to person #2 from the other team so they can take it back to their team. "Count up the number of happy faces written on the cards and praise or reward for use of happy statements.

Teams Share:

Read Alphabet Trees

Teams pair up to show their tree and read their sentence to another team.

Group Discussion:

Debrief the Lesson

Find out how the teams felt about the lesson by having them discuss in their teams the following:

- What did you enjoy about making the team tree?
- How could your team work even better next time?
- Can you think of another fun message to write on a tree?

Other Applications:

- Create a tree with a message for the principal.
- Create a tree with a message for a story book character.
- Create a praising tree with a happy message for the members of another team.

Extensions:

- Students write stories that tell what happens when the president received the alphabet tree.
- Teams plan and act out a skit that shows the president receiving the alphabet tree.
- The students decide what the president should do when he receives each of the messages.
- Have the students watch the newspaper and news broadcasts for current issues that would be appropriate to use for an alphabet tree message.

Variations:

- For kindergarten students, the teacher visits teams and writes the message while the students cut out the leaves.
- Older students write a longer message by putting several trees, each containing a sentence in their picture.
- Rotating Reporters read the tree message. Each student is a reporter once to a different team.

The Alphabet Tree

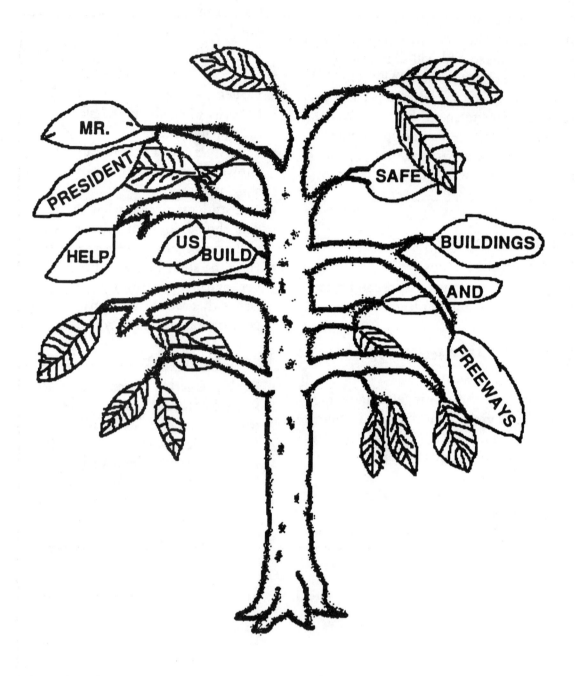

Happy Talk Cards

Clever Clusters

Lesson 34

• Literature

Swimmy

• Grade Level
1-2

• Type of Lesson
Writing Skills: Descriptive
Shape Cluster

• Cognitive Objective
Students brainstorm descriptive words
for a story character, and create a
shape cluster with the words.

• Social Skills Objective
Everyone Participates

• Materials
Large paper for the fish cluster, ditto sheets of red fish, one black fish per group,
scissors, colored markers and pencils.

- **Cooperative Project**
- **Group Discussion**
- **Roundrobin**
- **Signaled Sequential Roundtable**

Structures

Background Information

Students have heard or read the story *Swimmy* by Leo Lionni. As a class or in teams, they have developed lists of descriptive words about fish to assist them as they create their shape cluster.

Lesson Sequence

Cooperative Project:

Setting Up Supplies

Students meet in their teams. Each team is given several sheets of dittoed red fish, one black fish, a large background paper, marking pens and pencils.

Signaled Sequential Roundtable:

Choose and Write Descriptive Words

Using Signaled Sequential Roundtable, students take turns suggesting a descriptive word and writing each word on a separate fish, getting a thumbs up signal from the team. They continue until time is called.

A. The Importance of Everyone Participating

"You can help each other get ideas as you do Roundtable, but it is important that everyone contributes a word when it is his turn, because we are going to evaluate how each team does in having everyone in their team participate during the lesson."

B. Group Discussion: Preparation of the Shape Cluster

When the groups have all written at least three to four words per person in about ten to fifteen minutes, each teammember is to write their name on the front of his or her fish and cut them out. The group creates a fish shaped cluster out of the team's fish, adding in the black fish for an eye. When they agree upon an arrangement, each teammember glues their own fish on to the background sheet.

Group Discussion:

Everyone Participates

The group decides if everyone did their part by brainstorming, writing, cutting, and gluing their fish into the team's fish shaped cluster. Everyone who did their part signs the bottom of the team's cluster sheet. The class can validate each team's evaluation by counting the signatures on the individual fish in the shape clusters.

Roundrobin:

Debrief the Lesson

Teammembers take turns discussing any of the following questions to find out how the students felt about the lesson.

- How was it helpful for you to have a group to work with while you thought of descriptive words?

- What did your team do to make it easy for everyone to participate in making the fish?
- What did you enjoy as you worked with the team today?

Variations

Kindergarten students can do this lesson, but they don't add descriptive words to the fish. Their objective is to arrange the little fish into one big fish. They can then make up a story about an adventure their "big fish" has. All group members can help tell the story to the class

Other Applications:

- Shape clusters can be made to match other story characters.
- Cut-outs of little red dogs to make Clifford.
- Pigs for Charlotte from *Charlotte's Web* by E.B. White
- Mittens or kittens for *The Three Little Kittens* by Paul Galdone.

Extensions:

- The teams can create a new fish and make a shape cluster for it.
- The teams can create a new adventure for the fish in their shape cluster. They are to use words from their cluster in the new adventure story about their fish.

Fish for Shape Cluster

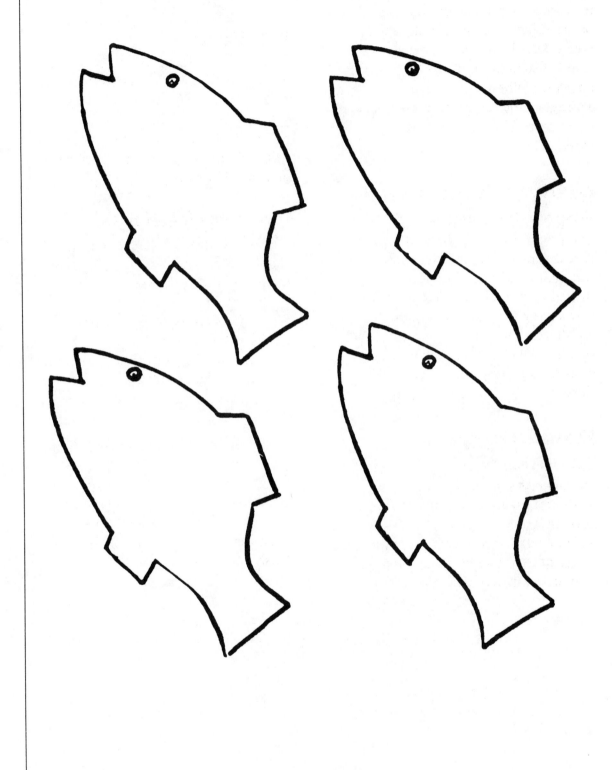

Stretch-A-Sentence

Lesson 35

• Literature
Animalia

• Grade Level
1-2

• Type of Lesson
Writing Skills: Descriptive Sentences

• Cognitive Objective
Teams of students take turns adding words to a base sentence which consists of an article, subject, and verb.

• Social Skills Objective
Active Listening

• Materials
Stretch-A-Sentence Sheet, Alphabet team identification cards.

Structures
- *Class Discussion*
- *Group Discussion*
- *Sequential Roundtable*
- *Rotating Reporters*

Background Information
Students will have had initial instruction in adjectives and several lessons using descriptive words in sentences. A suggested book rich in the use of adjectives is *Animalia* by Graeme Base.

Lesson Overview
"Students, today your team will choose a base sentence and you will each take turns adding a descriptive word for the sentence until time is called. While you study your cards, use quiet inside voices."

Lesson Sequence
Cooperative Project:
Write a Descriptive Sentence

Class Discussion:

A. Brainstorm Base Sentence Ideas
"Our base sentences today will be like the following:
- We like ice cream.
- We like dogs.
- We like cookies.

What are some other things we like?" List the ideas the students contribute.

B. Model Doing Build a Sentence
Choose three or four students to be a demonstration team to model how the Stretch-A-Sentence sheet is done.

C. Choose the Base Sentence
Give the teams a couple of minutes to discuss what base sentence they would like to use. Give the Silent Signal.

Sequential Roundtable:

Writing Words Descriptive

"In just a minute, person #1 will write the base sentence the team agreed upon on the base sentence line at the top of the paper. Then person #1 writes a descriptive word in box #1. The paper is passed to person #2 who writes a descriptive word in box #2. Continue passing the Stretch-A-Sentence sheet around the circle so everyone can write a descriptive word in their box each time the paper comes to them. The team may help by suggesting descriptive words. Continue to work until I ask for Active Listening."

Finger Evaluation:

Use of Inside Voices

After the students have worked for a couple of minutes, ask for Active Listening. "Students, think about the kind of voices your team has been using. Discuss how your team did in using quiet voices and decide whether your team should have a five because everyone used a Six-Inch Voice, or a three because most of the team used a Six-Inch Voice, or a one because they worked on the sentence but forgot about using a Six-Inch Voice."

"The person who has the answer sheet in front of them, count up the number of fingers your teammembers are showing and write that number in the top left corner of the paper." While they are counting and writing, ask some of the students to validate their score by explaining why they chose the number they are showing. "Continue to work on the sentence using your quiet, Six-Inch Voices."

Roundtable:

Continue To Build a Sentence

Let the students work until everyone has had one turn and most students have had two turns. Give the Silent Signal for everyone to stop adding words and pass the paper to person #6 who will write the sentence with all the descriptive words in it on the bottom line of the paper."

Finger Evaluation:

Use of Inside Voices

"While person #6 writes the sentence, we are going to vote on how well our team did on using inside voices. Pass the paper to person #5 who will count up the fingers and write the score in the top right corner. Look at the two scores. If your team got more points on the second score than they did on the first score, give yourselves a silent cheer for trying hard and improving."

Group Discussion:

Practice Reading the Sentence

"Take a minute and read over the sentence several times so everyone is comfortable reading it."

Rotating Reporters :

Read Descriptive Sentences

To identify each team, pass out Alphabet Letter Cards in order around the room. "Teams, it is now time to share your sentences. I will say two numbers. 'Numbers 2 and 4.' Students in each team with those numbers will be reporters and will go to the team with the next letter of the alphabet. The two of you will read the sentence to that team."

When they finish sharing with that team they rotate around the room to the next team and share again. After students 2 and 4 have shared twice, they return to their teams. Students 1 and 3 then share twice to two new teams.

Evaluate the Cognitive Objective
Collect the Stretch-A-Sentence papers to see that everyone contributed descriptive words for the team sentence.

Group/Class Discussion:

Debrief the Lesson
Have students discuss the following questions to find out how the teams felt about the lesson.

- How did the team decide which base sentence to use?

- Was it easy or hard to think of descriptive words for your team's sentence?

- What made it easy to share the team's sentence?

Extensions:

- Each student builds a different sentence using the descriptive words produced in the Roundtable.

- Teams exchange Stretch-A-Sentence papers and use that team's stretch sentence in a story they create.

- Teams exchange Stretch-A-Sentence papers and they try to add two more descriptive words to the sentence.

- Teams make pictures that illustrate other teams' stretched sentences.

Stretch-A-Sentence

Base
Sentence _____

1 _____

2 _____

3 _____

4 _____

5 _____

6 _____

Sentence _____

Lorna Curran: *Lessons for Little Ones: Language Arts*©
Kagan Cooperative Learning • 1 (800) Wee Co-op

Spell & Show

Lesson 36

• Literature
The Cat in the Hat
Brown Bear, Brown Bear,
What Do You See?
A House Is A House For Me

• Grade Level
1-2

• Type of Lesson
Writing Skills: Spelling

• Cognitive Objective
Groups of students decide together
how to spell familiar words from
stories they have read.

• Social Skills Objective
Polite Suggestions

• Materials
Chalkboards, chalk, erasers.

Structures
- *Class Discussion*
- *Numbered Heads*
- *Group Discussion*
- *Stand and Share*

Background Information

The students are familiar with the words they are going to spell because they have read them in their stories many times, and/or have seen them used many times in class stories and charts. This lesson is best used with stories that have easy words, that repeat themselves many times within a story, so the students are very familiar with the words. Examples are: *The Cat in the Hat* by Dr. Suess; *Brown Bear, Brown Bear What Do You See?* by Bill Martin Jr. and *A House Is A House For Me* by Mary Ann Hoberman. The class is familiar with making polite suggestions and has a chart of positive suggestions to review before starting the lesson.

Lesson Overview

"Your team will listen to a word I say. It will be a word that we have read and used in class many times. Together you will agree on how it should be spelled. Each person will write the word on their chalkboard. When I call out a number, the person with that number from each team will share the word. As we make suggestions on how to spell the words, we will use polite statements."

Lesson Sequence
Numbered Heads Together:

Spell Words From Story

A. Preparation for Numbered Heads
Teams of four students meet and number off from 1 to 4. Each team member is given a chalkboard, chalk, and an eraser.

B. Directions for Heads Together

"In a minute, I'll tell you a word. Your team is to talk over how you think the word would be spelled. When your team agrees on how to spell the word, everyone writes it on their small chalkboard. Remember to use polite statements as you make suggestions for the spelling of the word."

C. Group Discussion: Agreement on Spelling

"Spell the word cat." Watch as they discuss the spelling, agree on the spelling, and write the word on their chalkboard. Listen to and record the polite statements you heard.

Curran's Comments:

This lesson works best if the teacher forms groups which contain at least one student who finds it easy to spell correctly. That student can be a tutor to the other students in the group. If all group members use that students advice as they write the words on the chalkboards, then teams can be assured success.

D. Stand and Share:

Teams Show Answers

"Person #3 stand and show your chalkboard to the class. Check the spellings and compliment the teams for correct spellings and spellings that make sense, for example, "kat".

Emphasize the Polite Statements

Share any polite statements you heard. Praise to the teams that used polite statements.

Continue Using Heads Together

Continue giving them words to spell. Assign the sharing task to different people each time.

Group/Class Discussion:

Debrief the Lesson

Find out how the students felt about doing this lesson together by discussing these questions.

- What made it easy to spell the words?
- How did the polite statements help make today's lesson enjoyable?

Variations:

- The teacher says a letter sound or blend, and students write the letters that make that sound.
- The teacher says part of a rhyme and the students agree upon a word or words to complete the rhyme.
- The teams make up the words for the other teams to spell instead of the teacher giving the words that are spelled.

Extensions:

- The teams use the spelling words to write a group story to be shared with the other teams. Teams form Inside-Outside circles and tell their stories to each other, but stop each time they come to a spelling word and ask the members of the other team to spell the word.
- Individuals stand in Inside-Outside Circles with spelling words on flash-cards. They drill each other, then trade cards before rotating to a new partner.

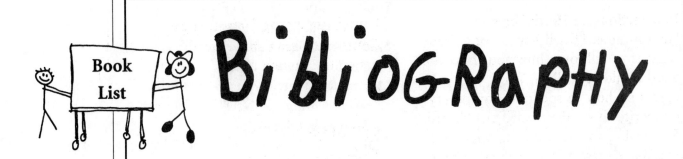

BIBLIOGRAPHY

Ahlberg, Janet and Allan. *The Jolly Postman.* Little Brown and Company, 1986.

Anno, Mitsumasa. *Anno's Alphabet.* Harper Collins, 1975.

Asch, Frank. *Happy Birthday Moon.* NY: Prentice Hall, Books For Young Readers, NY, 1982.

Base, Graeme. *Animalia.* New York: Harry N. Abrams Inc., 1986.

Brett, Jan. *Goldilocks and the Three Bears.* New York: Dodd, Mead and Company, 1987.

Bridwell, Norman. *Clifford the Big Red Dog.* New York: Scholastic Inc, 1985.

Brown, Margaret Wise. *Big Red Barn.* Addison–Wesley Publishing Co., 1956.

Carle, Eric. *The Mixed Up Cameleon.* Harper and Collins, 1984.

Carle, Eric. *Do You Want To Be My Friend?* Harper and Row, 1987.

Carlstrom, Nancy. *Jesse Bear, What Will You Wear?* New York: Macmillan, 1986.

Charles, Donald A. *Time To Rhyme with Calico Cat.* Chicago: Childrens Press, 1978.

Charlip, Remy. *Fortunately.* New York: Four Winds Press, 1964.

Cauley, Lorinda. *The Cock, The Mouse, And The Little Red Hen.* New York: G.P. Putnam's Sons, 1982.

Cohen, Miriam. *Will I Have A Friend?* New York: Macmillan, 1967.

Cole, William. *Poem Stew.* New York: Harper Collins, 1981.

Degen, Bruce. *Jamberry.* New York: Harper & Row Junior Books, 1986.

dePaola, Tomie. *Tomie dePaola's Mother Goose.* New York: G.P. Putnam's & Sons, 1985.

Dunn, Phoebe and Judy. *The Animals of Buttercup Farm.* New York: Random, 1981.

Ehlert, Lois. *Planting A Rainbow.* New York: Harcourt, Brace, Jovanovich Publishers, 1988.

Emberley, Ed. *Green Says Go.* Boston: Little, 1972.

Flack, Marorie. *Ask Mr. Bear.* New York: Macmillian, 1968.

Feeling, Muriel. *Hambo Means Hello.* Dial Books, 1974.

Fox, Mem. *Hattie and the Fox.* New York: Bradbury, 1986.

Gag, Wanda. *Millions of Cats.* New York: Putnam & Sons, 1988.

Gibbons, Gail. *Farming.* New York, Holiday, 1988.

Galdone, Paul. *Cinderella.* New York: McGraw Hill Inc., 1978.

Galdone, Paul. *The Three Little Pigs.* New York: Ticknor & Fields of Houghton Mifflin Co., 1979.

Galdone, Paul. *The Three Little Kittens.* New York: Ticknor & Fields of Houghton Mifflin Co., 1986.

Haskins, Ima. *Color Seems.* New York: Vangard Printers Inc., 1974.

Hoban, Tana. *A.B See.* Greenwillow, NY, 1982.

Hoban, Tana. *Twenty Six Letters and 99 Cents.* Greenwillow, NY, 1987.

Hoberman, Mary Ann. *A House Is A House For Me.* New York: Puffin Books, 1987.

Hoff, Syd. *Who Will Be My Friends?* New York: Harper Collins, 1985.

Hutchins, Pat. *Rosie's Walk.* New York: Macmillan, 1968.

Kitchen, Bert. *Animal Alphabet.* New York: Dial Books, 1984.

Lee, Douglas. *Animal ABC.* Milwaukee: Stevens Garreth Inc., 1985.

Leer, Edward. *ABC Alphabet Rhymes for Children.* Topsfield, Massachusetts: Salem House Publishers, 1986.

Lindbergh, Reeve. *Midnight Farm.* New York: Dial Young Books, 1987.

Lionni, Leo. *The Alphabet Tree.* From a collection, *Frederick's Fables, A Leo Lionni Treasury of Favorite Stories.* New York: Pantheon Books, 1985.

Lionni, Leo. *A Color of His Own.* New York: Knoph Books, 1993.

Lionni, Leo. *Fish Is Fish.* New York: Knoph Children's Paperback books, 1974.

Lionni, Leo. *Frederick.* New York: Knoph Books For Young Readers, 1967.

Lionni, Leo. *Little Blue, Little Yellow.* New York: Astor Honor, 1959.

Lionni, Leo. *Swimmy.* New York: Pantheon Books, 1963. New York: Knoph Children's Paperback books, 1987.

Lobel, Arnold. *On Market Street.* Greenwillow, NY, 1981.

Lobel, Arnold. *Frog and Toad Are Friends.* New York: Harper Collins, 1985.

Locker, Thomas. *Family Farm.* New York: Dial Books, 1988.

MacDonald, Suse. *Alphabetics.* Bradbury, 1986.

Martin, Bill. *Brown Bear, Brown Bear, What Do You See?* New York: Henry Holt & Company, 1983.

Miller, Jane. *Farm Alphabet Book.* New York: Scholastic Incorporated, 1981.

O'Neill, Mary. *Hailstones and Halibut Bones.* New York: Doubleday, 1989.

Pallotta, Jerry. *The Icky Bug Alphabet Book.* Watertown, MA: Charlesbridge Publishing, 1986.

Peek, Merle. *Mary Wore Her Red Dress.* New York: Clarion, 1988.

Prelutsky, Jack. *Read Aloud Rhymes for the Very Young.* New York: Knopf, Alfred A. Incorporated, 1986.

Rogasky, Barbara. *Rapunzel.* New York: Holiday House Incorporated, 1982.

Samton, Sheila. *Beside the Bay.* New York: Philomel Books, 1987.

Sendak, Maurice. *Where The Wild Things Are.* New York: Harper Collins, 1988.

Serfozo, Mary. *Who Said Red?* New York: Macmillian, 1988.

Shaw, Nancy. *Sheep In A Jeep.* New York: Houghton Mifflin, 1986.

Shultz, Charles. *Snoopy's Book of Color.* New York: Western Publishing Company Incorporated, 1987.

Suess, Dr. *The Cat In The Hat.* New York: Random House, 1957.

Testa, Fulvio. *If You Take A Paintbrush.* New York: Dial Books, 1986.

Ungerer, Tomi. *Cricktor.* New York: Harper Collins, 1983.

Waber, Bernard. *Ira Sleeps Over.* Boston Massachusetts: Houghton Mifflin, 1984.

Ward, Cindy. *Cookie's Week.* New York: G.P. Putnam's Sons, 1988.

White, E, B. *Charlotte's Web.* New York: Harper Collins Child Books, 1974.

Wildsmith, Brian. *Brian Wildsmith's ABC.* Salt Lake City, UT: Franklin Incorporated, 1963.

Winthrop, Elizabeth. *Shoes.* New York: Harper and Row, 1986.

Yashima, Taro. *Crow Boy.* New York: Puffin Books, 1976.

Yoshi. *Who's Hiding Here?* Natick, Massachusetts: Picture Books Studio, 1991.

Zolotow, Charlotte. *Mr. Rabbit and the Lovely Present.* New York: Harper Collins, 1962.